The 2R Manager

Peter E. Friedes

Foreword by David H. Maister

The 2R Manager

When to Relate, When to Require, and How to Do Both Effectively

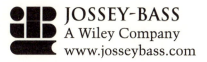

JOSSEY-BASS
A Wiley Company
www.josseybass.com

Published by

JOSSEY-BASS
A Wiley Company
989 Market Street
San Francisco, CA 94103-1741

www.josseybass.com

Copyright © 2002 by John Wiley & Sons, Inc.

Jossey-Bass is a registered trademark of John Wiley & Sons, Inc.

Jossey-Bass books and products are available through most bookstores. To contact Jossey-Bass directly, call (888) 378-2537, fax to (800) 605-2665, or visit our website at www.josseybass.com.

Substantial discounts on bulk quantities of Jossey-Bass books are available to corporations, professional associations, and other organizations. For details and discount information, contact the special sales department at Jossey-Bass.

We at Jossey-Bass strive to use the most environmentally sensitive paper stocks available to us. Our publications are printed on acid-free recycled stock whenever possible, and our paper always meets or exceeds minimum GPO and EPA requirements.

Jossey-Bass also publishes its books in a variety of electronic formats. Some content that appears in print may not be available in electronic books.

Library of Congress Cataloging-in-Publication Data

Friedes, Peter E., 1941-
  The 2R manager : when to relate, when to require, and how to do both effectively / Peter E. Friedes ; foreword by David H. Maister.
      p. cm.—(The Jossey-Bass business & management series)
  Includes bibliographical references and index.
  ISBN 0-7879-5893-X (alk. paper)
  1. Communication in management. I. Title: TwoR manager : when to relate, when to require, and how to do both effectively. II. Title: When to relate, when to require, and how to do both effectively. III. Title.
  IV. Series.
  HD30.3 .F75 2002
  658.4'5-dc21

                                                              2002004709

FIRST EDITION
PB Printing   10 9 8 7 6 5 4 3 2

The Jossey-Bass

Business & Management Series

To managers who want
to realize their own potential
by helping others realize theirs

—ᴍ— Contents

—⚬— Foreword

Peter Friedes knows and understands things about managing that most of us struggle a lifetime to learn. At last, with this book, he is sharing his insights with a general audience.

I first encountered Friedes in 1980 when, as an assistant professor at the Harvard Business School, I went to Hewitt Associates to write my first case study on a professional service firm.

What I saw was an organization with a strong people orientation, applied equally from shareholders to support staff. I saw a place that had the courage to choose people for different roles according to their skills, not their rank. In some operating groups, owners who excelled at professional tasks but were not necessarily suited to be managers were reporting to nonowners who were excellent managers. Unusual for its time (and perhaps even today), Hewitt did not make use of profit centers by offices or services but successfully created a culture of cross-boundary collaboration termed "The One-Firm Firm."

Yet working at Hewitt Associates was no cakewalk. As I was informed by various associates, junior and senior, during my interviews, hard work was expected. The central challenge of the case study I wrote was to ask the reader whether Hewitt Associates could maintain its values and culture while continuing to raise its productivity and financial performance. The case study proved to be a litmus test of beliefs. The "Requirers" in the classroom could not believe that success could be built on a foundation of concern for employees as human beings. The "Relaters" loved what they saw but were skeptical, fearing that commercialism would destroy the culture. They were both wrong. Hewitt's ever-increasing success showed that the two sets of skills and approaches not only *could* be melded but *must* be melded.

In twenty years of consulting to and writing about professional service firms, I learned that the Hewitt approach has general applicability. Its focus on managing people well, eliminating internal boundaries to serve clients better, and adhering to the highest professional standards are the hallmarks of great firms in every profession. Attention to managing the culture, and not just the financials, has been an indicator of success that I learned at Hewitt but have observed repeatedly since.

I never did find out who created Hewitt's culture, but I know who sustained it, nurtured it, and grew it: Peter Friedes. He was my first teacher (and hero) in the rudiments of running a professional firm and may still be the best. Everything I learned about professional firms was based on insights and frameworks that he generously shared with a young academic.

Now it's your turn. Read on. Think. Absorb. And act. We are all lucky to have access to the wisdom contained in this book.

Boston   DAVID H. MAISTER
April 2002

⎯⎯ᴧᴧᴧ⎯ Preface

Throughout my twenty-three years as CEO of Hewitt Associates,* I tried to find or create more effective ways to develop managers. What fundamental skills do our best managers have that others don't? How do we assess the varying beliefs, attitudes, and behaviors of existing managers and then help each of them manage better?

Retirement allowed me the time and perspective to focus on the questions that really interested me. When I was asked as a consultant to improve the process of peer review and coaching for all Hewitt Associates' managers, I saw something I should have seen years earlier that provided answers to these questions with unusual clarity.

Managers have naturally either a Relating or a Requiring style. Those who naturally require are weaker at relating—sometimes much weaker—and vice versa. The best managers possess the ability to do both well and know when to choose one over the other. These highly versatile managers carry out traditional management functions intuitively. They think beyond immediate assignments. They face issues and problems with creativity, compassion, and resolve. What I came to see is that Relating and Requiring are *fundamental* skills for effective managing.

---

*Hewitt Associates is one of the largest human resource consulting firms in the world, with over thirteen thousand associates generating over $1.7 billion in annual fees from eighty offices in thirty-one countries. While I was the CEO from 1970 to 1993, our income grew at an average annual rate of 23 percent. In addition, we were named as one of the "100 best companies to work for in America" by authors Robert Levering and Milton Moskowitz, starting in 1984 and continuing in every updated edition during my tenure. It features an unusually strong organizational culture of cooperation among individuals, practices, offices, and regions.

The ability to relate is crucial in that it helps managers understand their direct reports better, use their skills more effectively and receive the benefit of their people's ideas and natural motivation. But it's possible to have too much of a good thing. Extreme Relaters need to be liked so much that Requiring is threatening to them, so they routinely avoid the confrontational aspects of coaching for and insisting on excellence.

Requiring, too, is imperative for every manager. In an age of increasing accountability, managers need to ensure that timeliness, quality, and productivity goals are met. Of course, Requiring can also be taken to counterproductive extremes, resulting in managers who have to dominate and expect people to do things their way. As a result, extreme Requirers are unable to demonstrate sufficient Relating skills to garner their people's ideas and retain their motivation.

What we need is 2R training to help managers know when to relate, when to require, and how to do both effectively. In 1999, I developed and led a half-day course for thirty managers to help them recognize their natural management style in terms of Relating and Requiring. Their response was enthusiastic. Managers quickly picked up on whether they were more naturally Relaters or Requirers, gained revealing insights about the impact they were having on the people they managed, and knew what they needed to do to become more effective. I then ran the course for over a thousand Hewitt Associates managers. The course and the feedback I received from it led to this book.

The 2R Manager will help you become a better manager. Unlike other management books, it offers specific advice tailored to each individual's current management style. You will take some tests, see the results, and learn the impact you now have on the people you manage. You'll learn what changes you must make to become more effective. That's the relatively easy part. The tough part is actually taking the steps to improve. To help you do that, we'll examine why you resist improving some of your less natural skills and how you can overcome this resistance. Then you'll be free to understand, accept, and practice how to make the necessary changes. *The 2R Manager* walks you through this developmental process.

In fact, the 2R concept is so easily understood that you may tend to run through it too quickly. You will encounter statements or questions that should make you want to stop and take a few minutes to reflect. You will have some "aha" moments when it suddenly becomes clear why you or your employees behave in certain ways. I would encourage you to keep a highlighter handy, because you will want to return to those insights after you have learned even more about yourself. Although the book will only take a few hours to read, it will suggest avenues of growth for years. After reading it, you won't have fifty things to do, just one or two important skills to develop with explicit steps to get started and a personal set of checklists, techniques, passages, and chapters to refer to.

Although the book may initially seem oriented to the new or relatively new manager, it is equally applicable to the experienced or senior manager. Management versatility (the ability to work differently with different people and situations) has not been taught well. Experience can help overcome that, but most managers have evolved a particular style (with its strengths and weaknesses) and pretty much stick to it. In the training courses I ran, it was the senior managers who were the most surprised by how much they learned. Having more experience that validated the concepts, they understood that they'd missed being trained in versatility and needed to pick it up quickly to achieve their goals.

Over time, I've refined the 2R process to the point that it should help any manager in any environment. Managers from the newly appointed to the CEO are not optimizing their effectiveness when they cannot access both Rs. Every kind of organization faces similar "human relationship" challenges. The path to improvement lies in helping existing managers become 2R managers who have the ability to relate and require as needed.

There are many good management books already in print. Some are comprehensive textbooks; some give you a dozen or a hundred good ideas. Many have particular specialties, such as coaching. Others are parables with good messages. But no other book gives you more personal insight regarding how you manage now and how you can improve and then shows you how to do so.

No doubt people will come to this book with a variety of purposes and interests. Some of you may want to transform the management culture of your companies. Others may be young managers interested in advancing your career by becoming better at your job. Still others are HR people intrigued by a training alternative that can help reduce time and costs. *All* of you will find what you're looking for in *The 2R Manager,* and you'll discover tools, techniques, examples, and ideas that will help you implement this process in your work life and your organization.

This book is a practical guide to human behavior in the workplace and to getting the best from the people who work for and with you. My hope is that you will enjoy this exploration of your beliefs, behaviors, and impact on others and will make the most of the opportunity to become better at what you do.

Winnetka, Illinois   PETER E. FRIEDES
April 2002

The 2R Manager

2Rs Are Better Than 1

The 3Rs are the foundation of American education. Reading, 'riting, and 'rithmetic are the building blocks on which all advanced learning depends. Even if a student is brilliant in math and knows his future is in this field, he is expected to become proficient in reading and writing. No matter what a student's most "natural" R might be, she is taught the other two on the assumption that one way or another, they will be needed. The brilliant mathematician, for instance, may be able to convince his colleagues that his new theorem is correct because he is able to write a clear, persuasive paper on the subject. While he may lean on his math skills to make his reputation, he must also access his reading and writing capabilities to further his career and perform his job more effectively.

The 2R system serves a similar function for managers. To be a good manager today, you need the versatility to *relate* to the people you manage and to *require* that they produce results. Of these 2Rs, one is going to be more natural for you than the other. The trick is learning how to use your less natural R, when needed, to acquire the versatility of a 2R manager and the increased effectiveness that comes with it.

THE PROBLEM WITH BEING
A 1R MANAGER

Managerial performance suffers when people get locked into one style. All of us are Relaters or Requirers to varying degrees. At the extreme, the Requirer acts like a drill sergeant when she should be collaborating, whereas the Relater is trying to be his subordinate's best friend when he should be setting deadlines and goals. Most managers don't operate at the extreme—they are not 100 percent Relater or Requirer—but they are overly reliant on their natural style. They are so dependent on that style, in fact, that they deny themselves access to a range of problem-solving ideas and effective approaches. Many managers operate at significantly reduced capacity by ignoring or infrequently using their less natural style.

Jack, for instance, was a young brand manager with a Fortune 500 company. He had a sterling pedigree—Harvard M.B.A., two years with a top consulting firm, and three years of glowing performance reviews. Jack was known in the company as someone who met deadlines, brought projects in on budget, and possessed superior marketing skills. During his first three years with the company, he was rotated through a series of staff assignments and consistently came up with problem-solving ideas. Because management had tabbed him as a high-potential employee, he was expected to perform well in his first-time managerial position.

It wasn't that Jack performed poorly in this position. His first assignment, introducing a line extension, went well. Jack crafted an innovative strategy and worked with his people and the company's ad and sales promotion agencies to create a splash. After a solid test-marketing program and rollout, however, a competitor introduced a similar product with lowball pricing that began eroding Jack's company's share. Jack responded by riding his people and his agencies hard to develop a plan to regain market share. When they didn't come up with anything he found suitable after a few days, he took on the assignment himself, working round the clock for a week to devise a new strategy. Although his direct reports liked aspects of Jack's plan, they also noted some glaring flaws. Two of his people, who had worked on the brand for a number of years and were more familiar with the market than Jack was, pointed them out. But Jack brushed them aside and refused to entertain a discussion of the issues they had raised.

When the strategy was implemented, it didn't live up to Jack's or the company's expectations. Just as significant, Jack had quickly created a bad relationship with his direct reports, who were convinced that their boss wouldn't listen to their ideas unless they agreed with his own. His inability to use a Relating style when it was needed damaged his relationships, thereby causing his people to withhold ideas and information in the future.

If Jack doesn't learn to use his other R, he won't be on the fast track for long. Either negative feedback from his people will reach Jack's boss, or his group will lose talented individuals. Careers are derailed when managers fail to learn to use their other R.

Essentially, people like Jack are managing with one hand tied behind their back. Like just about every manager, he is capable of drawing on both Relating and Requiring styles. The problem, of course, is that most managers reflexively apply their dominant style, especially in times of stress. If they're Relaters dealing with a crisis situation, they automatically try to relate their way out of that crisis, rarely considering a Requiring solution. It's as if they have a blind spot that keeps them from seeing other possibilities.

Managers who are more versatile can choose from a much greater spectrum of alternatives. In a workplace where versatility is becoming increasingly important, this is a major advantage. Unfortunately, traditional management training does not focus on versatility. Instead, it tries to help managers learn each of the different functions that make up managing, usually in discrete modules.

TOO MUCH INFORMATION, NOT ENOUGH TIME

It's difficult to train managers effectively in an environment where they have less time and more to do than ever before. Years ago, managers did most of their learning on the job over long periods of time, observing their bosses in action. These informal apprenticeships allowed them to pick up skills incrementally, an appropriate training approach in that they were given increased responsibility at a slow, measured pace.

Today, with many managers barely more experienced than the people they manage, there is no time for slow, or even fast, apprenticeships. To accelerate learning, numerous types of training may have become part of a manager's daily life. You may have attended sessions on an assortment of topics, from communication, decision making, leadership, or project management to diversity, team-building, e-commerce, performance appraisal, compensation, or something else. A host of techniques, including coaching, brainstorming, risk-taking outdoor adventures, distance learning, and computer simulations may have been used to help you. But how much has the learning process really been accelerated?

Just about every company is concerned about rising training costs and the lack of return on that investment. Developing managers by creating discrete training modules for each management function is too slow. With so many topics, organizations are forced to select the most vital ones, leaving important gaps. There's too much for managers to absorb in the time they and their organizations are willing to devote to it. Perhaps more important, the training is often not designed to adapt to the beliefs, attitudes, and behaviors of existing managers.

HEARING WHAT YOU BELIEVE, TUNING OUT WHAT YOU DON'T

People hear best the ideas that reinforce what they already believe. If you are naturally a Relater, you readily absorb the Relating messages in a training session (or in a workshop, lecture, or book). The instructor might talk about the need for managers to be supportive of their direct reports and learn to empathize with them. Upon hearing the instructor make this comment, a Relating manager might say to herself, "That's a good point. I should regularly ask my employees if they are doing well and how I can help them do better." A Requiring manager might hear this same message and think, "Give me a break! I'm the manager here. It's wimpy to ask your employees how they feel all the time."

Let's turn the scenario around and consider how a Requirer might respond to a Requiring-friendly message. In a training session on project management, the instructor stresses that it's crucial to build in project checkpoints designed to assess employee progress at various stages. The Requirer says to himself, "Good reminder. In every project, I should incorporate these checkpoints so that I can assure that my employees are on target to produce the quality we need." A manager who is a natural Relater, however, might hear this message and think, "I trust my people. I'm not going to let them know I think they can't get it right by insisting up front that they continually check in with me."

We each hear different things from the same words depending on our belief systems. Messages have to pass through our filters to be heard, and unless we are versatile, these filters block the messages from being understood as they are meant. The problem with traditional training is that it does not distinguish between the Relaters and Requirers in the room. It sends the same message to both.

Let's say an organization wants to help a group of managers improve their decision-making skills. The Requiring manager, comfortable with her own judgment, generally makes decisions easily. Because she feels she has the answer, she is often eager to tell others why the group should go in a certain direction. Her decision-making weakness, however, is her tendency to decide too fast. She should be advised to slow down and to get (and be open to) input from others to make better decisions.

On the other hand, the Relating manager generally wants other people's ideas before making a decision but then hears conflicting opinions from his direct reports. Since his tendency is to procrastinate, allowing the conflicting views (and the resulting disagreement when he makes a decision) to delay the decision, he should be trained to make a decision sooner—not by majority rule, but by what he feels will best achieve his group's goals.

Clearly, these two individuals need to receive very different messages to become more effective managers, but the decision-making curriculum assumes that one message fits all. Managerial training in many organizations is not tailored because trainers have underestimated the grip our natural styles have on our managerial behaviors and our ability to listen. The solution is to first acknowledge that managers are Requirers or Relaters and then structure the training with these two styles in mind. By recognizing a manager's natural style and asking her to adapt, rather than ignoring it and asking her to change, the training will more effectively accomplish its goals.

A MISSING LINK

Some companies attempt to offset unimessage training by offering personality or communication style tests to increase self-awareness. Myers-Briggs, for instance, is a well-known personality test that helps determine if you are introverted or extroverted, intuitive or sensing, thinking or feeling, judging or perceiving. By studying your particular profile (out of sixteen possible profiles), you can gain significant insight into your personality.

Another approach to help managers gain self-insight involves a communication style test such as the one found in *The Art of Managing* (Hunsaker and Alessandra, 1986), which divides people into Expressives, Drivers, Analyticals, and Amiables. These tests are a popular way to illustrate different and distinct communication styles. They are especially useful to understand why you have conflicts with individuals who use opposing styles.

Some consultants have used the Myers-Briggs and communication style test results to create management development courses, with some positive results. The insight gained helps you understand how to communicate better with people who have different styles from yours. However, the successes would be greater if there were a way to overcome three limitations:

- The tests do not directly test managers' relationships with the people they manage. Instead, they test personality or communication style.

- To avoid sounding too critical, an attempt is made to tell everyone that no matter what his or her personality or communication type is, it's OK. As managers, however, they are not all OK; most have minor negative impacts, and some have severe ones.

- The connection between what you learn about your personality or communication style and what actions you should take to manage better is unclear. For example, let's say your communication style is Expressive. After learning the impact Expressives have on others, what should you do differently to get better results from your people? Are you supposed to be less expressive as a manager?

By overcoming these limitations, the 2R system represents the next logical step in managerial training. The tests are specifically about your actions and behavior with your employees. The results may show that your style is not effective in many situations. And most important, the connection between the insights you will gain and the actions you must take is a strong one, easily understood and intuitive. The insights you gain will be about how you now relate and require. The actions you must take to become a better manager will be to relate and require effectively, as dictated by the situation. The 2Rs provide a missing link between insight and action so that you can achieve more of what you want as a manager. By increasing your versatility to use both Rs, you'll not only get more out of training but also increase your managerial effectiveness to the point that you've already achieved what the training was designed to confer.

VERSATILITY: A SHORTCUT THAT WORKS

Ideally, all new managers would take a course that would teach them about Relating and Requiring styles, identify their dominant style, and help them become more versatile so that they can shift to that less natural style when the situation calls for it. This basic training would make any other subsequent type of training much more effective. Instead of tuning out training messages that went against their natural style, managers would open their minds to these ideas. In a communication course, for instance, the Relater would not automatically resist learning how to talk to direct reports about deadlines to ensure they're met, and the Requirer would not automatically resist learning how to talk empathically with direct reports in an attempt to see their point of view. Because they are being trained to be 2R managers right from the start, more information would be heard, more alternative solutions considered, and more problems solved.

Because most people lack this basic training, the 2R system functions as a tool to retrain managers. Every manager at every level needs to evaluate his current penchant for Relating and Requiring and transform his style to increase his versatility. You should understand, however, that the more you are locked in to a particular style, the more challenging this task may be. Managers can become very comfortable with their natural style and resistant to hearing messages that conflict with the inherent truths of this style. Overcoming that resistance is facilitated by certain common situations managers find themselves in. Let's look at two.

Awareness that their natural style is no longer as effective as it once was

Going back to basics is easier if clear evidence exists that being a Relater or a Requirer is creating problems in the current environment that didn't exist before (or weren't major issues in the past). Kim, for instance, was a forty-one-year-old senior manager with an accounting services company that had done extraordinarily well for the past fifteen years. Kim had been with the company for thirteen of those years, and her relating style dovetailed with the company's laid-back culture. Recently, however, the company's fortunes had taken a turn for the worse, and there was increasing pressure on all senior managers for results. In the past, Kim's boss had encouraged her to be a bit tougher with her people, but she had not taken his suggestion very seriously. Her new boss, however, made this same suggestion more emphatically, and Kim was acutely aware that she had to get better performance out of her key people. As a result, she was more willing than in the past to question her Relating style and attempt to draw on a Requiring approach at times.

Observing that some managers with different styles can easily accomplish tasks that they find difficult

Sometimes you observe, even in managers whose style you don't like, that they can do some things with their reports that you find very difficult to do. The Requiring manager can ask for what he wants, for example, and can easily set deadlines and priorities. The Relating manager communicates very easily with her people. You see these skills in a manager whose style is different and know if you could tap in to your less natural style, you would be significantly more effective.

Ultimately, retraining a manager using the 2R method recalls the following adage: Give a man a fish, and you feed him for a day; teach him to fish, and you feed him for a lifetime. It is more helpful to the manager to teach him to use both Rs than to give him a seemingly endless series of training courses on every management subject. If he knows his 2Rs, he will perform every managerial function better. Knowing when to relate versus when to require is relevant whether you're trying to motivate one of your people to work harder or attempting to solicit reactions to a tentative conclusion you have reached. A versatile manager is a better communicator, a better decision maker, and a better consensus builder than his 1R counterpart. Anyone who knows how to use both styles will, like the skilled fisherman, know how to provide for himself and his team in all sorts of situations.

THE PROCESS OF BECOMING AND STAYING VERSATILE

Why can't you just tell a manager who is primarily a Relater that she needs to take greater advantage of her Requiring style and a Requirer that he must use Relating skills at appropriate times? Because our Relating and Requiring styles have psychological roots that aren't easily changed through verbal suggestion. To understand why we need to change, we need to accept that what we're doing isn't always working and that we're a big part of the problem. It's relatively easy for most people to admit that they should make greater use of the opposite R. What stops them is knowing how. It's not just a matter of exercising willpower and making an effort to exhibit their less natural R behaviors. Instead, it's a four-step process of *self-assessment, style familiarity, increasing versatility,* and *situational implementation.* These steps coincide with the four parts into which this book is organized.

The *self-assessment* phase, covered in Part One, will help you locate yourself on the Relating-Requiring matrix. Using questions about your activities and behavior, you'll be able to pinpoint this location. Because people aren't pure Relaters or Requirers, each style has a number of gradations. Whereas it's relatively easy to identify your dominant style, it's not as easy to determine how strong your Relating drive is versus how weak your Requiring drive is (or vice versa). The more precisely you pinpoint this mix, the easier it will be to address what changes need to be made.

Part Two deals with *style familiarity.* Many managers cling to one style because they believe it's what makes them effective or it's what feels comfortable to them. As a result, they have difficulty letting go and becoming more versatile. In this part, we'll explore some of the myths and misconceptions that keep managers overreliant on one of the Rs. As you'll discover, the more you understand the ramifications of each style, the more motivated you'll be to learn how to shift between styles, based on the dictates of a given situation.

Part Three focuses on *increasing your versatility* as a manager, a challenge for many but a realistic goal for most. We'll begin by defining what versatility is and isn't within a 2R context. It's not about achieving a 50–50 balance between relating and requiring but rather about learning how to switch between styles at appropriate moments. Achieving versatility is more difficult than it might seem, since people's attitudes often militate against switching styles. We'll examine the attitudes that favor and fight against versatility and the types of attitude adjustments that managers should make. A critical portion of this discussion involves exercises and other prescriptive tools designed to help managers become more versatile. I'll provide "interim" steps that will help managers move toward a more versatile stance. (Relaters, for instance, need to take the interim step of becoming more assertive, while Requirers must take the step of becoming more attentive.)

In Part Four, on *situational implementation,* I'll concentrate on how to use and maintain versatility in the daily role of managing. It is easy to slip back into a dominant style when faced with the daily pressures or when you're in an unfamiliar setting (after being promoted to a new job, for instance). In this final part, you'll find a variety of common scenarios portrayed and advice on how to maintain your versatility in each.

Although this four-phase process is straightforward and easy to read, it will take some introspection and openness to understand the effect you have on others and how you can increase your behavioral options. The payoff, however, is significant. By the time you've finished this book, you'll know exactly what you need to do to become an infinitely more effective 2R manager. The first step is to pinpoint whether you are a Relater or a Requirer. This is the subject of Chapter Two.

PART ONE

Self-Assessment

Identifying Your Natural Style

I magine this chapter not as writing on a page but as a mirror. Imagine further that it's a special kind of mirror—a management mirror. As you read and do the suggested exercises, you'll find your management style reflected back. Instead of your image, you'll see your management behaviors, warts and all.

The purpose of this mirror is to help you identify your most natural behaviors and the distinct style they add up to. To that end, you'll find two surveys. One focuses on how much you *relate* to your employees, the other on how much you *require* of them. Based on your answers, you'll receive a score for both your more natural style and your less natural style. You'll be able to check these scores against descriptions of Relating and Requiring managers. If the descriptions and the scores agree, you will know your natural style. If they do not agree or if you're skeptical about what the scores suggest, a few additional tools are provided to help you pinpoint whether you're a Relater or a Requirer.

SURVEYING HOW YOU MANAGE NOW

Rate each statement according to how you actually act with the people you manage, not on how you think you should act. (To get maximize value from this book, you must be as honest and objective as possible in your assessments of how you now manage your employees.)

RELATING SURVEY

This survey contains twenty statements about you as a Relating manager. On the line to the right of each statement, write the number that best reflects the extent to which each statement is true of you. Indicate how you *actually* act with the people you manage: 1 = to little or no extent; 2 = to some extent; 3 = regularly; 4 = to a great extent.

1. I include my employees in the decision-making process. _____

2. I look for ways to encourage the people I manage. _____

3. I want my people to like me. _____

4. I am available to listen to what they want to say to me. _____

5. I accommodate my people who have important personal issues that conflict with working. _____

6. I share messages, memos, business e-mail, and other information as I receive it. _____

7. I have a friendly demeanor toward my people. _____

8. I ask my employees how they like the job. _____

9. I involve my direct reports to help me think through problems and issues. _____

10. I spend time thinking about how I can help each of them grow. _____

11. I enjoy teaching them what they need to do. _____

12. I coach each individual on how he or she can improve. _____

13. I know the strengths, weaknesses, potential, and interests of each person who reports to me. _____

14. I compliment my people when I observe good work. _____

15. I think about my relationship with each of my employees. _____

16. I empathize with my people. _____

17. When someone makes a mistake, I view it as a
learning opportunity. _____

18. I know if someone is overworked and talk with that
person about what we can do about it. _____

19. If a direct report has a problem, he or she knows I will
try to help. _____

20. I try to cooperate rather than compete with other
departments in the firm. _____

Circle the *five* lowest numbers among your responses. Add up the
remaining fifteen numbers and place the sum on this line: _____

REQUIRING SURVEY

This survey contains twenty statements about you as a Requiring manager. On the line to the right of each statement, write the number that
best reflects the extent to which each statement is true of you. Again,
indicate how you *actually* act with the people you manage: 1 = to little
or no extent; 2 = to some extent; 3 = regularly; 4 = to a great extent.

1. It is important to me that my unit exceeds expectations
in the eyes of my managers. _____

2. I expect my people to do whatever it takes to complete
a job well. _____

3. I set clear and definitive expectations for evaluating
performance. _____

4. I follow up on projects given to direct reports to assess
if they're on track or if they need redirecting. _____

5. When an assignment is not completed to my satisfaction,
I ask the person to redo or improve it until it meets my
expectations. _____

6. When someone arrives late often, socializes during work,
makes a lot of personal calls, or in other ways takes
advantage of flexibility given, I address the issue. _____

7. I stretch good performers to take on new responsibilities
even if they aren't sure they are ready. _____

8. I try to complete every request no matter how much is already "on my plate." _____

9. I am clear about our priorities with my people. _____

10. I address recurring performance problems. _____

11. I make very efficient use of my time. _____

12. I make sure that my direct reports make very efficient use of their time. _____

13. I have a lot of ideas about what things should be done and how they should be done. _____

14. I accept that conflict will exist if we are to accomplish our goals and do not worry about that. _____

15. I meet with new people to describe our mission and communicate my expectations. _____

16. I insist on receiving high-quality work from each person. _____

17. I am comfortable giving honest feedback about how the individual is doing. _____

18. I enjoy judging how people, projects, and assignments are going. _____

19. I am comfortable making decisions. _____

20. I communicate the importance of meeting deadlines. _____

Circle the *five* lowest numbers among your responses. Add up the remaining fifteen numbers and place the sum on this line: _____.
Transfer the results to the following summary:

	RELATING RESULTS	REQUIRING RESULTS
Copy the total from each survey:	_____	_____
Divide each number by 6:	_____	_____

This calculation converted the scores to a 10-point scale, where 10 is high. The higher number of your two scores reflects your *preliminary* natural style.

To begin understanding your results, think about your score versus what you would consider ideal. For instance, if someone gave himself a 4 ("to a great extent") for each of the fifteen statements, he would receive a score of 10 ($15 \times 4 = 60 \div 6 = 10$). If someone recorded a 2 for each statement, she would receive a score of 5 ($15 \times 2 = 30 \div 6 = 5$). What two scores for Relating and Requiring do you think reflects the "ideal" manager? Is 10-10 the perfect manager? Would you prefer to have a 6-6? Let's look at what the numbers signify.

Interpreting Your Scores

On the Relating survey, all of the statements concerned Relating behaviors that if done regularly will lead to a caring and trusting relationship with employees. If you gave yourself a 3 for each activity (for an overall score of 7.5), you would be doing an excellent job of establishing a respectful, nurturing relationship with each of your people. Overall, if you scored between 7.0 and 8.0, you are relating about right. Such a score would signify that you are a people-oriented, caring manager. If you answered that you do many of these activities to a great extent (a 4 answer), your desire to make others happy is probably having a negative effect on your managerial effectiveness. The more 4s you have, the more difficult you'll find it to use Requiring actions when needed. In essence, you'll find versatility more of a challenge. A 4 may seem better than a 3 to you for a given statement; for instance, you believe that including direct reports in the decision-making process "to a great extent" is better than doing it just "regularly." The problem comes when you record 4s for several statements, because this signifies that you are working too hard to relate. If you answered with 1s and 2s, you are not regularly doing these caring, helping activities and probably find Relating difficult.

The same basic interpretive principles apply to the Requiring survey. Again, the statements all represent Requiring that if done regularly will lead to getting the best results from your people. If you gave yourself a 3 for each statement (for an overall score of 7.5), you are likely ensuring high-quality work. Overall, if you scored between 7.0 and 8.0, you are demanding results in an appropriate way and are a task-oriented, Requiring manager. As with the Relating side, the more 4s you give yourself, the more you're locked in to this style and the more difficulty you'll have being versatile. The more your total score

rises above 8.0, the more likely you are to experience a negative impact on your effectiveness and success as a manager. If you answered
with 1s and 2s, you are resistant to these Requiring activities and rarely
put them into practice.

I should add a qualifier to your Requiring score. In the workplace,
getting quality work from your reports involves more than the actions
a manager takes. As you've probably witnessed or experienced first-
hand, even if you're doing all the Requiring activities regularly, you
can't guarantee quality work. Your tone and manner might not be appropriate. You might say the wrong things, articulating what must be
done in a demeaning way. You might base your requirements on false
assumptions, or your people might not be capable of carrying out
their assigned tasks. Although you cannot be in full control of the results, you are in control of your actions and can learn to optimize
them for the best chance of success.

Thus the optimal score for both surveys is between 7.0 and 8.0.
Such an average would mean that you would have the ability and comfort level to relate or require, as necessary, with each person you manage. Remember, though, that even if you score between 7.0 and 8.0,
this doesn't mean that you have a "neutral" style—there is no such
thing! If your score is higher in Relating or Requiring, the higher score
is an indication of your natural style.

Finally, I want to emphasize that even though 10 typically signals
a perfect score in our culture, it is not a perfect score here. For instance, ideal Relating managers don't relate incessantly and obsessively.
They observe the boundaries between themselves and their employees; they understand that at some point they need to take a step back
and trust people to act on their own. When managers relate too
much—even if this relating involves caring, asking, and listening
behaviors—the boundaries are violated. In many cases, the neediness
of the over-Relating manager affects people's behavior negatively (for
example, direct reports start to do and say things to meet their boss's
psychological needs). From a psychological standpoint, the 10-score
Relating manager creates a dysfunctional relationship with his people.

In the same way, so does the Requiring manager who has a 10
score. It's possible to require regularly but allow a certain amount of
discretion to each employee. Managers who require at the optimal
level don't constantly look over people's shoulders and make them feel
distrusted. When managers require at the 10-level, two bad things happen. First, their people come to regard them as control freaks who

enjoy exercising power for power's sake. The harder these managers push, the more resistance they encounter. Second, overly Requiring managers seem not to respect their people; they communicate that they don't trust them to get things right on their own and that the only way they will get things right is if they follow the boss's orders.

You may find yourself wondering if your direct reports or your manager would agree with your survey results. In "More Resources for the 2R Manager" at the back of the book, I have included another survey you may want to use with your employees, along with some comments and cautions about using them. Because ratings at all levels are influenced by how Requiring and Relating the raters are, you will not be able to get a purely objective rating. My experience is that as long as you have honestly indicated to what extent you actually do each activity noted on the surveys, the results will be an accurate reflection of your management style. However, let's make sure that the numerical results match the descriptive evaluations of Relating and Requiring styles.

DOES THIS SOUND LIKE YOUR NATURAL STYLE?

Now that you know whether you scored higher on the Relating or Requiring survey, you can assess which description of the two styles is closer to how you think and act as a manager. I'll provide an idealized description of each type of manager and then some of the more common behaviors associated with each style. Recognizing that you exhibit some traits from each of these two styles, my goal is to help you identify which style is more natural to you.

The Ideal Relating Management Style

This type of manager focuses on establishing a good working relationship with each person he manages, believing that a good relationship is necessary in order to work effectively and achieve good results. In many instances, Relating managers are motivated by an ideal: they want to help others succeed. As a result, they provide guidance designed to facilitate strong performance.

Because Relating managers are intent on fostering individual growth, they want to help each direct report reach his or her potential. This means encouraging an employee when he needs encouragement, supporting him when he needs support, and coaching him when he needs coaching. It also means being flexible if there is an unusual personal issue that requires your employee's attention, recognizing that each person has a personal life with its own demands. Ideal Relating managers don't just do and say what satisfies the immediate needs of their people. Their approach is longer-term and more substantive: not only do they want to help their direct reports succeed in their current jobs, but they also want to prepare them for future roles. Nurturing their skills and competencies is one way to prepare them.

When direct reports make mistakes or fall short of expectations, Relating managers handle the situation in a future-oriented rather than a blame-oriented manner. They help the employees see the consequences of their behaviors, especially in terms of the effect it will have on them (and the group) in the future. Learning from mistakes, constructive criticism, and objective discussions about what went wrong are all part of this approach. Relating managers feel good about themselves when they establish solid relationships and help their people succeed.

ACTIONS THAT IDENTIFY RELATING MANAGERS. Of course, most Relating managers do not match the ideal. In practice, the behavior of Relating managers may include some of the characteristics listed here. (Note that at this point, you should avoid judging these actions as good or bad, ideal or less than ideal. What is important is to determine if the descriptions for one style fit your behavior more or less than those for the other style.)

- Shies away from conflict and confrontation or avoids giving negative feedback to their reports
- Asks questions of people to discover how they think and feel
- Exhibits more team-oriented than individually competitive behavior
- Sees the people issues in policy discussions
- Expresses more empathic comments than judgmental ones
- Dislikes employees who are very sure of themselves and highly opinionated; views these people as "strong" but also inconsiderate of others

- Worries about being liked and is very averse to criticism (giving or receiving it)
- Has a tough time telling people that things need to be completed quickly and should have priority; will take on additional work personally rather than press others to help
- Becomes quiet around people he or she disagrees with or dislikes; usually doesn't take these people on

The Ideal Requiring Management Style

This type of manager focuses on results, achievement, quality, accuracy, innovation, service, and profitability. Requiring managers believe that it is necessary to carefully monitor quality in order to achieve it. Getting the task done right is a mantra, and these managers insist that work be redone if it's wrong. They concentrate on setting and meeting both deadlines and goals. They delight in exceeding their boss's expectations and take pride in working hard and personally achieving significant objectives.

Their coaching is aimed at improving the work product rather than the person. Requiring managers deal quickly with poor or marginal performances. They set high standards, especially for creative problem solving, accuracy, clarity of written and oral communication, timeliness, and thoroughness, and they coordinate well with others to get better results than any one person can achieve. All of these standards have a positive intent—to get the tasks done well and on time. Accomplishment is what makes Requiring managers feel good about themselves, and they often talk easily and confidently about their accomplishments.

ACTIONS THAT IDENTIFY REQUIRING MANAGERS. As with Relating managers, most Requiring managers do not match the ideal. In practice, typical behaviors of Requiring managers may include the following:

- Communicates great faith in his or her ideas, decisions, vision, and so on
- Acts as if he or she has the answers and resists asking questions of others
- Competes as an individual rather than as part of a team

- Acts distant and aloof and prefers completing tasks to conversing with people; doesn't care much about being liked
- Believes that every second counts and doesn't equate relationship building with getting work done
- Makes priorities clear and is concerned if a job isn't being done well or fast enough
- Experiences difficulty in asking questions and waiting for the answers before expressing his or her opinion
- Takes on too much work, believing that he or she can do it better than direct reports can

At this point, you may have confirmed that your scores fit with the descriptions and know whether you are more naturally a Requirer or a Relater. If so, you can skip the next section. If not, read on.

TOO CLOSE TO CALL

There are several reasons why you may not yet be confident about which is your more natural style. It is likely that your scores for Relating and Requiring are so close that you see aspects of yourself in both descriptions without knowing which is more dominant.

Please take the following "clarifying" test. Begin by looking at the behaviors listed in group A and group B. Decide which group is *further* from how you behave as a manager. Let's say that after reading group A, you feel that you exhibit only a few of the listed behaviors. After reading group B, however, you feel that you never exhibit *any* of those behaviors. This would mean that group B is the further from how you behave as a manager.

Group A

- You take over in group or individual meetings a lot. You interrupt or finish others' sentences.
- You push others hard—often trying to do the impossible.
- You're stubborn—it is hard for others to change your mind.
- You feel that others don't speak out or volunteer ideas (perhaps for fear of being interrupted or criticized).
- You direct others and know what should be done in most situations.

- You tell others your agenda and don't show much interest in listening to your employees' agendas.
- You require or confront others using words that are harsh, strong, or judgmental of the person.
- Employees have told you that you behave insensitively toward them.
- Employees have told you that you act arrogantly about your own abilities and opinions.

Group B

- You feel responsible for your employees' success or failure.
- You have such a great need to be liked that you find yourself trying to please employees on every interaction. You show sensitivity to their feelings and don't want to leave them feeling bad about anything.
- You are continually asking your employees how they feel and if everything is OK.
- You are so empathic and understanding about how it feels to be confronted about performance issues that you avoid confrontations.
- You may delegate to a fault—leaving employees to do tasks on their own.
- You accommodate your employees at the expense of getting the work out on time and with the highest quality.
- You have a tough time defining priorities because you believe it will usually result in some disagreement or argument.
- Employees can change your mind quite easily, even if you were fairly sure that you wanted to pursue a certain course of action.
- You continually monitor your employees' reactions to what you're saying.

Choose the grouping that is further from your behavior as a manager. If it is group A, you are closer to being a Relating manager. You may not do many of the extreme Relating items in group B, but the Requiring extremes listed in group A are further from how you behave. If group B is further from how you manage, you are closer to being a Requiring manager, even if you don't do many of the extreme behaviors on the list.

At this point, some of you may still feel that equal parts of both styles apply to you. You find all the traits listed in groups A and B equally nonreflective of how you manage. It's as if for every Requiring trait, you possess an equal and opposite Relating trait. See if any of the following descriptions sounds like your actions:

- You are more task-oriented than relationship-oriented but do not find it easy to require of others.

- You have high standards but have trouble imposing them on others.

- You are very assertive upward toward your managers but much less assertive downward.

- You are more people-oriented than task-oriented but are able to make demands of others.

- You are good at building relationships but are not an especially good listener.

- You are very task-oriented personally but neither relate to nor require of others easily.

- You perceive of yourself as a versatile manager but don't like spending the time that Relating calls for or dealing with the conflicts that Requiring creates.

If one or more of the these seemingly contradictory pairings of traits describe you and your dominant style is still too close to call, here is a simple tiebreaker: Add up the five scores for the responses you circled (your lowest five scores) from your Relating survey and then your Requiring survey. Whichever sum is higher reflects your more natural style.

BEFORE YOU MAKE ASSUMPTIONS
BASED ON YOUR NATURAL STYLE . . .

Even though you are now reasonably certain what your style is, don't jump to additional conclusions that seem logical but may be wrong. Let's look at some of the common misconceptions that arise after people determine whether they're a Relater or a Requirer.

First, keep in mind that a manager isn't exclusively one or the other of these two types. Every manager is a hybrid. Even the most Draconian of managers might be good at relating to his bosses. Even the most humanistic of managers might be good at demanding that her people get the work done during crisis situations. Therefore, don't worry if your natural style isn't "pure."

Second, neither style is better than the other. Excellent managers can be natural Relaters or natural Requirers. They become excellent by becoming versatile.

Third, your natural style is unlikely to change. While it's theoretically possible to change a Requirer into a Relater (or vice versa), it isn't likely to happen. That's because these styles are rooted in our childhood experiences; one approach makes us more comfortable and helps us get what we need psychologically. The goal of this book isn't to change your natural style but rather to make you more versatile so that you can access the other style on occasion. Being versatile, however, doesn't mean that you're going to use Relating and Requiring in equal proportion.

Fourth, don't assume that you've incorrectly identified your natural style because this is a self-administered assessment. "If a manager isn't very self-perceptive in the first place, how will he come up with the right self-assessment in this test?" is a common question heard in management training workshops. Although a manager might not be perceptive about the effect she has on others, she will know if she is or is not engaging in the specific actions noted in the forty statements on the surveys. It doesn't require perspicacity to determine if you are performing specific actions; perception is needed only when it comes to understanding the impact those actions have on others.

However, if you want to seek confirmation of your style from your employees, there is a survey you can use in "More Resources for the 2R Manager" at the back of the book. This survey consists of twelve statements for your employees to rate that will reveal how they see your leanings toward Relating or Requiring behaviors.

The forty survey statements provide the basis for understanding how much you relate to and require of the people you manage. Although you now know which style is more natural to you, you do not yet know how much you favor your more natural style and how much you resist your less natural style. The next two chapters will help clarify this so that you can be placed in the most appropriate category on the following matrix:

REQUIRING

	LOW	ABOUT RIGHT	HIGH
LOW	Low Relating, Low Requiring	Low Relating, About-Right Requiring	Low Relating, High Requiring
ABOUT RIGHT	About-Right Relating, Low Requiring	About-Right Relating, About-Right Requiring	About-Right Relating, High Requiring
HIGH	High Relating, Low Requiring	High Relating, About-Right Requiring	High Relating, High Requiring

RELATING

CHAPTER THREE

About-Right Requiring for Requirers

Now that you know if you're more naturally a Relater or Requirer and have some understanding of each style, you can begin to become a 2R manager. The intent of Chapters Three and Four is to help managers use their most natural style about the right amount, while understanding their opposite style better, as preparation for becoming versatile 2R managers.

The primary objective of Chapter Three is to talk directly to Requirers about how to use their Requiring style most effectively, neither too little nor too much. Using one's natural style the right amount is a prerequisite for developing the versatility to use one's less natural style when needed. The secondary objective is to have Relaters "overhear" the messages in order to begin to reduce their resistance to Requiring and to learn how to work more effectively with Requiring people.

Chapter Four then talks directly to Relaters about how to use their Relating style the right amount while Requirers "overhear" the messages in order to begin to reduce their resistance to Relating and to learn how to work more effectively with Relating people.

LOW REQUIRING (UNDER 7.0): INCREASING YOUR REQUIRING ACTIONS

People sometimes assume that all Requirers are cut from the same cloth: they ride people hard, set unrealistic expectations, and find fault with anything less than perfect performance. In fact, one natural Requirer may be quite different from another. For instance, if your score on the Requiring survey was 6.9 or less, you are a low Requirer. You are not implementing a Requiring style enough to "do regularly" all the activities described in the Requiring survey. Because requiring is easier for you, it may seem paradoxical that you don't do it sufficiently. The paradox makes sense, however, when you realize that you are likely to be overly involved in *doing your job* and not sufficiently involved in *being a manager.*

Ravi is a manager at a transportation services company who spends the vast majority of his day at a keyboard. Ravi is a whiz, valued by his organization for his software design contributions, but because he places relatively few demands on his people, they are not performing anywhere near his level. As a result, he's working an absurd number of hours each week while carrying his group on his shoulders. When he has the time to manage, Ravi is great at setting deadlines for his people and providing them with the resources necessary to meet goals and do solid work. Unfortunately, Ravi gets so caught up in his software design projects that he neglects to use his natural managing style.

If you are low in your Requiring behaviors, you are not insisting that all jobs delegated are being done well. That is the place to start. Check the status of all the work your direct reports are doing. Follow up as necessary to ensure that their work is meeting your standards. Once you accept that you are not doing this task sufficiently, it should not be hard to correct because it fits your Requiring mind to want to get more good work from your people. The trouble is that you are often distracted by what you want to do more. You undoubtedly pride yourself on the quality of your own work. As a manager, however, you need your group to accomplish more. If the only way to do it is for you to work harder, you will run out of hours to give (if you haven't done so already). The only logical answer is for you to get more help from the people you manage.

Select your best person, and ask her to help you more. What part of your job can you share with or assign to her so that she can assume some of your workload? Write out a step-by-step developmental plan for her to take over this part of your job. Once you have worked with one person to get more help, that success will spur you to continue the idea with all the people you manage.

Another approach is to look at the statements on the Requiring survey that you rated 1 or 2. Some of these would be easy for you to do more frequently. Put them on your to-do list every day, and check each one when you accomplish it, but don't cross them off completely for a month. Commit to retest yourself on the Requiring survey at the end of the month to verify that these changes have moved your Requiring behaviors toward the "about right" category.

HIGH REQUIRING (OVER 8.0): DECREASING YOUR REQUIRING ACTIONS

If your score on the Requiring survey was 8.1 or more, you are a high Requirer. Occasional excesses in your style are leading to unwanted outcomes. If your score was 9.0 or more, the likelihood of negative impacts on the people you manage is very high.

You need to understand in a new, deeper way that by taking your style too far, you're hurting your chances of achieving the results you want. This understanding may come hard, especially since your style worked for you in the past and was probably why you were promoted to a managerial position in the first place. There's a big difference, however, between the qualities prized in an individual contributor and those valued in a manager. As a manager, you will be evaluated in part on how you develop others. You need other people to mature in their roles, to feel good about themselves, and to stay with you and contribute.

Be aware that your perfectionist, results-oriented nature may foster an environment where you must constantly watch over everything to get it right. You will be the victim of a self-fulfilling prophecy: others won't volunteer to do things differently or better because they know you will ultimately take over the project and direct how you want it done. Your extreme oversight dampens their initiative. By not enabling others to feel good about their own accomplishments and ideas, you diminish their incentive to maximize their contribution.

When faced with these observations, some Requiring managers become defensive. The protests are usually one of two variations on the same theme. Some Requirers feel that they were taught to be demanding, perhaps by watching a demanding parent do what seemed to work. Others believe that if you want to have work done really well, you have to demand it. Of course, both these observations have elements of truth in them. But they cannot be used to excuse *overly* Requiring behaviors. The impact of over-Requiring diminishes the benefit gained by being a Requirer in the first place.

For example, Rick had a father who was "the boss." Dad was in charge of the family, and Rick and his two older sisters knew it. They learned to obey, and the family was very close. Rick envied his dad's power, admired his certainty, and grew up like him. Not surprisingly, Rick had trouble when he became a manager. The strength of his belief that he had all the answers left his direct reports stunned. Rick's managers were sufficiently concerned that they brought in a coach to help him learn how to communicate better with his people. Though Rick understood what the coach was telling him and recognized that she was making valid points, he had no basis in his past experience for knowing how to change. Everything he had witnessed was now being questioned.

Of course, the old command-and-control paradigm in work environments long ago lost popularity in favor of a more participatory, democratic model. Corporate cultures now value qualities like empathy and influence along with decisiveness and authority. This doesn't mean, however, that Requiring is no longer a viable managerial style. Far from it. As I've emphasized, it's just as viable as the Relating style. An organization without natural Requiring managers is a company without good results. What's bad is the negative impact caused by excessive Requiring behaviors. To come to terms with this impact, look at the following list of over-Requiring actions and note the ones that might apply to you:

- Taking charge too much; not giving others enough rope (you may interrupt or finish their sentences)
- Pushing too hard and often trying to do the impossible
- Being stubborn (it is hard for others to change your mind, even if there is new information)
- Preventing others from speaking out or volunteering ideas because they fear you'll interrupt or criticize them (more likely if you manage people over a longer period of time)

- Being overly direct and encountering resistance from even good performers
- Being eager to tell direct reports your agenda but uninterested in listening to theirs
- Confronting others using words that are harsh, strong, angry, or judgmental
- Being insensitive to others or arrogant about your own abilities and opinions

As you consider this list, don't try to justify your managerial behaviors. You may have had very good reasons for being overly direct or stubborn. Instead, focus on the unintended reactions you provoke. Even if other factors contribute to these reactions, you are in part responsible and need to know when to tamp down your Requiring impulse.

What might help is to become aware of how others perceive you. Requirers are sometimes shocked to learn that their employees do not feel good about themselves when the Requirers are around. Here are some representative comments from people who have had managers who were excessively Requiring.

"I feel bad around him; he makes me angry and irritated, and I resist giving him anything more than I have to. He acts like he knows everything."

"It was oppressive. He belittled me. I wanted out of there."

"You learn to just give her what she wants, no more—no volunteering, no suggestions for improvement, even if you know they are good suggestions. Just get it done her way and move on."

"It sure isn't a team. It's do it his way. He doesn't listen to what you have to say. Over time, you say, 'Screw it.' I'll leave when I can."

"He keeps saying we've got to get it right, but he is the sole definer of *right.*"

"I learned something from my manager—he taught me what he wanted and he got it from me—but he wouldn't listen to my ideas of how to make things better and so I lost my commitment."

"It just hurts your self-esteem. No uplifting comments, no compliments, lots of criticism. It brings you down to work for an excessive Requirer."

"Everything I did was not good enough. Nothing would please the manager I had. I used to work very hard trying to please him until I saw how futile it was."

Do any of these comments sound like something your people might say about you? More to the point, do you understand how these reactions negate your effectiveness as a manager?

DECREASING YOUR OVER-REQUIRING TENDENCIES

To decrease your Requiring actions, consider the following ideas:

1. *Recognize the damage done by over-Requiring.* Some managers dismiss this damage because they underestimate the impact—not just the depth of it but also the breadth. Think about whether your actions may have triggered any reactions like these:

- Workers who fail to perform as well as you expect, who diminish their contributions out of anger, fear or spite
- Complaints about how you manage made to you or your boss
- Resentment of or resistance to giving you what you want
- High turnover in your group
- Inability to develop individuals in your group for managerial positions
- Difficulty in meeting group objectives
- Increased dependence on you to get work done the way you want it
- Job frustration because of employees who seem to lack motivation and don't respond to challenges
- Being assigned fewer people to manage
- A once-promising career that stalls because of some of these problems

If you've experienced some of this fallout, you understand that over-Requiring is hurting your career, your job satisfaction, your group, and your organization.

2. *Understand that over-Requiring is a habit.* You have developed a habit because it served you to do so. It may have helped you feel in control, feel more confident, or perform personally. The particular reason is not important. What is important is that you have not yet observed that the excessiveness of the habit is undercutting your success as a manager. You may have gotten input that it sometimes hurts you but still feel that the strengths of your style outweigh the problems.

3. *Be aware of the common rationalizations over-Requirers use to justify their actions.* When people question you about being too tough or demanding (or you question yourself in response to negative feedback), do you use any of the following rationalizations?

- My people won't get it right unless I review everything they do.
- I care about the quality of our work more than anyone else; this may cause some problems, but it's worth it if we turn out a top-notch product.
- My people might not like me, but they respect me.
- My style has worked for me all my life—it's helped me achieve what I've achieved—so why should I think it's not working now?
- I can work harder than anyone, and even if others don't contribute, I'll more than make up for their lack of effort.
- My job isn't to develop people—I'm not in human resources—but to deliver results, which I do.
- I may turn off some of my people, but others are inspired by my values and will do anything I ask.
- Today's employees—especially the younger ones—are cynical and lazy and won't perform unless they're pushed hard.
- If my employees would do what I tell them, they would do better work.

Recognize these rationalizations for what they are, and don't let them prevent you from decreasing your Requiring actions. It may be true that you can work harder than anyone or that some of today's employees are more cynical or less driven than those of a previous generation. Nonetheless, these circumstances still don't justify the negative impact your over-Requiring behaviors have.

4. *Learn to lighten up.* First, you need to lighten up yourself, and then you need to lighten up on others. Richard Carlson, in his books *Don't Sweat the Small Stuff—and It's All Small Stuff* (1997) and *Don't Sweat the Small Stuff at Work* (1999), offers hundreds of creative ideas to avoid taking everything so seriously. For over-Requirers, I've used the term *lighten up* to remind them that many issues, problems, and irritations do not necessitate a strong negative reaction. You have a perfectionist ideal about the way things *should be,* and you're in the habit of reacting when people and situations do not live up to the ideal.

You have more choices in how you react. If an event or situation is highly predictable, why get so upset each time it occurs? In everyday life, traffic is a perfect example. In managerial life, there are a host of predictable traffic jams or roadblocks to success. Accept that they will occur, get out of the strong-reaction habit, and learn to work around them. Phrases such as "roll with the punches," "go with the flow," and "whatever" are all used to accept reality. Avoid getting upset with an ordinary irritation.

If you lighten up on yourself, you will lighten up on others. Others will not see and respond to your anger and annoyances as much. Your increased ability to focus more on solutions will help the people you manage. And there is another thought that can help you lighten up on others. Understand that because you are known to be highly Requiring, your words are felt even more heavily than you mean them. Think of someone who might be intimidating to you. Perhaps it is a pro wrestler, a defensive lineman, a Nobel scholar in your field, or one of your parents. Imagine this person's face two feet from yours yelling at you. How might that feel to you? Keep that image in mind as you require with your people. You are the boss, an instant presence in every room, and even calmly demanding has an authority about it that you may not realize. If you can lighten up the words (and the body language that goes with them), you'll be more effective.

5. *Use games, devices, and tools to help you practice being lighter.* Since over-Requiring is a habit that developed over time, you need to find ways to reduce the excessiveness long enough to evaluate if you can achieve what you want without it. The following are some ideas— mental games, practices, call them what you like—to help you reduce excessive Requiring. Some are serious, and some are lighthearted attempts to get you to take yourself less seriously. Not all of these will feel right for any one person; select the ones that might work for you.

• Reduce "I" statements. Over-Requirers often use *I* when *we* would be more accurate and appropriate. This is a habit that you can catch yourself doing. Develop an ear to hear yourself using *I* or *my,* as in "my people," "my group," or "my goals." Use *we, us, our people, our group,* and *our goals.* This one item can work wonders for over-Requirers to create the sense that your group is a team.

• Play a game called "Will It Really Make a Difference?" This game is to take one of your over-Requiring activities and start every morning with the question, "Will it really make a difference if I don't do this activity today?" For example, will it really make a difference if I let everyone who talks to me finish the thought before I jump in with my comments? The good part of the game is the answer is almost always no. So don't do it.

• Can you find a symbol or an object that you stare at that has a calming influence on you? Whenever you are annoyed and about to criticize one of your people, bring the symbol to mind to calm you down so you can say what you want without the anger. This is especially useful to try before you call one of your direct reports or before you leave your office. For example, maybe a picture of your family or of a relaxing vacation spot (on your desk or in your mind) might encourage you to take a deep breath in stressful moments, which will enhance your effectiveness.

• Find a phrase or mantra for the activity you are trying to reduce. Say it when you get to work, after lunch, or at other easy times to remember. For example, one of the quickest ways a manager can convey to direct reports that she isn't stubborn is to occasionally change her mind. That sounds flip, but it is a serious point. Be on the alert for new information from your people that allows you to change your mind on a decision. Maybe you need a "stay open to new information" mantra; when you walk into your office or work area, say it four times.

• Pretend you are a performer in a soap opera. Your role has been to be a bossy, demanding tyrant. This week, however, the writers are developing your character, asking you to be more observing and contemplative.

• Imagine that you are an impartial observer judging yourself, giving "black and blue" points when you are over-Requiring and "silver and gold" points when you moderate your Requiring. Literally, keep score for a week, and see which colors win.

• Look at each statement on which you gave yourself a 4 on the Requiring survey. Ask yourself why you do this activity "to a great extent." Are you really doing it because you now think this is the best way to get what you want, or is it a habit that you can moderate? Reflecting on the reasons behind your over-Requiring behaviors will eventually help you decrease these behaviors. How might you do each of these activities differently to warrant a 3?

• Create a "go-to" alternative—what you might do instead of the activity where you over-require. Whenever you catch yourself about to over-require, switch to your "go-to" alternative. For example, if you are about to cut someone off and launch into one of your themes (which your conversation partner has heard before), can you ask a clarifying question about what your partner is saying instead?

• Play "Stretch It Out." Instead of doing the over-Requiring activity once a day, you move it to every other day for a week, then every third day, and so on. Just by recognizing it as an over-Requiring behavior, you will naturally reduce its frequency.

• Plan to take the test again a month from now with the intent to score closer to "about right." You are likely to be a competitive person who likes to win. Winning this game is doing all the requiring activities *regularly*, not "to a great extent."

Lightening up on these behaviors doesn't mean eliminating them. Insisting on excellence, challenging your people to stretch to achieve their goals, and meeting deadlines are all part of a good manager's job. The key is reducing the intensity of these common Requiring behaviors so that your people want to help you rather than resist you.

Remember, lightening up is the major strategy for reducing your over-Requiring tendencies. Reducing these tendencies is a prerequisite for increasing your versatility to relate more effectively. Work on it slowly and continually over a long period of time.

ABOUT-RIGHT REQUIRING (7.0–8.0)

If your score on the Requiring survey was between 7.0 and 8.0 and you do not identify with the low or high Requirer, you are probably Requiring in the right amount. You focus on results, achievement, quality, accuracy, and the productivity of your people without showing excessive anxiety or without exhibiting extreme behaviors. About-right Requirers regularly correct work, ask for it to be redone, and insist on excellence to ensure that all tasks assigned are done well and on time. They confront poor or marginal performers quickly to help them contribute at an acceptable level. If that can't be done, they encourage poor performers to leave the organization. They have a drive for completing tasks and achieving results but do so in a manner that is "group" goal oriented rather than "personal" goal oriented. They get cooperation for what they are trying to do rather than resistance.

It might be useful to ask yourself if you feel closer to being a low Requirer or a high Requirer, based on what you have read about them in this chapter. If necessary, review the tests to see if you gave yourself the benefit of the doubt on some survey items (for example, look at each of your 3s and assess if you leaned toward a 2 or a 4). As you add information about how much you relate, it will be helpful for you to understand any tendencies you have toward low or high Requiring.

Finally, when reflecting on your about-right score, think about how you might have responded to the statements differently if you were working under stressful conditions. Natural Requirers sometimes become even more results-focused and perfectionistic under pressure. They may be about right during "normal" times but over-Requiring when things get tough. While they may be diligent about soliciting ideas from their direct reports when things are going well, they may resort to rugged individualism in make-or-break situations.

You now have some feel for your natural R behaviors and how you might moderate them to require in the about-right range. You should be comfortable placing yourself in the broad groupings of low, about right, and high, though you may have some leanings within the grouping.

WHAT RELATERS MAY HAVE LEARNED

If you're a Relater, you'll benefit from what you just read in a number of ways. First, it's enormously helpful for managers to become familiar with the ins and outs of their less natural style. You may know some Requiring managers who fit the under- or over-Requiring descriptions and should now have a sense of what they need to do to be more effective.

Second, did you monitor your inner voice as you were reading about over-Requiring managers? Write down any specific thoughts or criticism you had about these managers, as that criticism gives you support to resist being more Requiring of your people. We will explore how to reduce your resistance in Chapter Eight. I hope you accept that all of the Requiring activities in the Requiring survey are ones that good managers regularly do. If you know some Requiring managers who do it about right, you probably admire how easily and guiltlessly they work with their people to insist on good work getting done on time. It is the excessiveness in Requiring that keeps Requirers from achieving their objectives, and it is the same excessiveness that you react to when you resist being more Requiring. Most Relaters don't want to behave like their view of over-Requiring people.

Third, you'll find knowledge about Requiring useful in dealing with both direct reports and bosses who are Requirers. Rather than getting angry at Tom's actions to be in control, you'll recognize that he is an over-Requirer who can learn to dilute this need. If Tom is your direct report, you will have sufficient insight into his behavior to help coach him in this direction. If Tom is your boss, you may or may not choose to coach him; perhaps reproducing, highlighting, and anonymously leaving him the relevant pages of this book might serve the same purpose.

Finally, the information here will enable you to pinpoint whether your Requiring category is low (under 7.0), about right (7.0–8.0), or High (over 8.0). The odds are that it's one of the first two.

About-Right Relating for Relaters

*C*hapter Three focused on helping Requirers require the right amount. This chapter is the flip side, helping Relaters relate the right amount.

LOW RELATERS (UNDER 7.0): INCREASING YOUR RELATING ACTIONS

If your score on the Relating survey was 6.9 or less, you're not actively doing your more natural Relating activities regularly. In 2R terminology, you're a low Relater. While it is possible that you have very experienced people working for you and feel you don't need to communicate with and help them to the degree you would with less experienced people, other explanations are more likely. One possibility is that you are trusting a lot; more likely, you are hoping a lot—that things go well without your asking, helping, teaching, or checking. You may not want to get close enough to know there are problems.

At Hewitt Associates, we've had many managers whose natural style is Relating but who prefer to spend their time consulting with clients.

Don, for instance, was a well-liked, friendly manager with four consultants working for him. He had an easygoing relationship with each of his people. The problem was that he didn't coach, oversee their work, or direct how they would grow. He hoped they would solve their own problems, much as he did when he was younger. Not surprisingly, the productivity and quality of work in Don's group didn't meet our expectations. Don attributed productivity weakness to the type of small project consulting his group did while continuing to be proud of his personal productivity numbers. When his manager stopped accepting the excuses and insisted on better managerial performance, Don needed to adapt his preferred approach.

Every organization has Relating managers like Don who avoid using even their natural Relating skills to manage because they love doing something else more. In that regard, they are like Requiring managers who under-require, as you will recall from Chapter Three. But there is an additional force that keeps under-Relating Relaters from managing more: not only do they like doing what they are doing personally, but they often don't like the activities involved in managing others. Managing requires them to confront performance, decide pay, set priorities, and shoulder other tasks that engender conflict, disagreement, and emotional reactions they don't want to deal with. They are repelled by these activities while being attracted to their personal work. These managers unconsciously adopt the technique of hoping and praying that their people will perform well.

If you find yourself hoping a lot while throwing your energies into nonmanagerial work, you may be a low Relater. Fortunately, there is a very direct approach to increasing your Relating that fits well with your natural skills. To get started, meet individually with each of your people; find out what they are doing, what problems they are having, and how you can help. If you show that you have renewed interest and will stay involved, you will quickly establish a stronger relationship with your people.

After you have caught up with what your people are doing, review all your circled statements on the Relating survey or the ones on which you rated yourself 2 or 1. Make a plan to do more of these activities with each of your employees. The goal is to do each activity on a regular basis.

For the activities that you feel are the hardest to do, note the major obstacles to increasing them. For instance, let's assume that one of the most difficult behaviors for you to do is to look for ways to encourage the people you manage. The obstacle you identify as preventing you from encouraging Jean might be "I know I will hear about how disappointed she was with her last raise." Next, come up with one or more actions to overcome this obstacle. For example, think about times in your own life when you were disappointed and how you had to talk it out and work it through before it was behind you. Then reach out and allow Jean to vent her concerns so that she can move past them and your relationship can grow. You know how to listen with empathy and understanding. This is a good place to do it.

This obstacle-action tool is useful whenever you know you should do something and know how to do it but notice that you are resisting doing it. Ask what is stopping you from doing it and what action might overcome the obstacle.

Unfortunately, even though my suggestions are simple and straightforward, they will often not be used. It is my experience that the biggest problem for Relaters who need to increase their Relating is wanting and committing to do it rather than knowing how to do it. Committing means that Don will have to accept doing less of what he loves in order to spend more time managing, which he doesn't love. That is very difficult for managers like Don to do. Unless Don is forced to make a conscious decision to manage more, he is likely to continue to manage minimally. This problem will be explored further in later chapters.

HIGH RELATERS (OVER 8.0): DECREASING YOUR RELATING ACTIONS

If your score on the Relating survey was 8.1 or more, you may be overly reliant on your Relating behaviors, creating problems for your people through excess. In 2R terms, you are a high Relater. If you scored 9.0 or more, it's especially likely that you're exhibiting behaviors that are making it difficult for direct reports to perform at peak efficiency.

In one sense, it's more difficult for high Relaters to recognize and respond to their style problems than it is for low Relaters. The latter have the quality but don't use it often, while the former use it too much. Consequently, high Relaters have trouble perceiving that there's a problem with their style, since Relating is a positive trait and they are exhibiting it constantly. Too much of a good thing, however, can be detrimental.

You can identify a high Relating tendency if you exhibit any of the following traits:

- You believe you are responsible for your direct reports' success or failure.
- You have such a great need to be liked that you find yourself trying to please your people on every interaction; you are very sensitive to their feelings and don't want to leave them feeling bad at the end of a conversation.
- When talking to your people, you are constantly trying to receive signals from them about how they feel about what you are saying.
- You guess a lot about what your employees think.
- You often ask a direct report how he or she feels and if everything is OK.
- You find reasons (that are not needed to conduct your business) to call your employees or visit with them just to be with them and feel close.
- You are so empathic and understanding about how it feels to be confronted about performance issues that you avoid such confrontations entirely.
- You are accommodating and nice to your people, sometimes at the expense of getting the work out on time with the highest quality; this often places extra burdens on you to complete their work or cover for them.
- You have a tough time defining priorities, for that will usually result in some disagreement or confrontation.
- Your people can change your mind quite easily, even if you were fairly sure of a desired course of action.

If some of these actions and attitudes apply to you, you are likely causing reactions from the people you manage that you do not intend. Jody, for instance, manages thirty-three full- and part-time employees in a mall clothing store. She feels enormous pressure to succeed and is committed to doing so through pleasing her employees, who will in turn serve the customers well. She works extra hours, but many of them are catering to her employees' wants rather than directing everyone's efforts toward achieving sales goals.

Scheduling her people is a daily example of putting her goals in conflict, as several people will complain to her about her initial schedule and others will complain if she revises it. Jody feels she walks on eggshells as she tries to direct their efforts or make decisions, often guessing which individuals will like or not like what she wants to do. She has lost some good people, is nervous about losing others, and often asks them if they like their job and how she can help them.

In essence, she has turned over the power in her relationships to her people. Of course, she isn't getting what she wants from them, but she'd be surprised to learn that her employees aren't getting what they want from her, either. As one of them said, "Jody is trying too hard to be my friend when what I need is a manager who will direct me and give the store direction [by making decisions and setting priorities]."

The "trying to be my friend" remark is telling. Employees often refer to high-Relating managers in this way. The following are the most common verbal reactions from people who feel they are working for high Relaters:

"It feels like you don't have a manager—you have someone trying to be your friend."

"It appears like the manager cares a lot about you, but you learn that the manager cares most about being liked by you."

"It isn't helpful—you don't get good, clear directions on the job, and you don't get any feedback on how to do better. He doesn't insist on other people's work being excellent, so how can we deliver excellent work?"

"It's real clear that my manager is uncomfortable with conflict."

"You don't grow and learn from this manager—he was too shy to give me any feedback."

"It becomes clear that you are in charge of the relationship, not the manager. She wants me to like her, and that need shifts the power to me."

"Priorities aren't set, conflicts and issues aren't resolved—it is not conducive to getting good work done."

"We waste more time getting nothing done; it's very frustrating."

"It is fascinating to me that what the manager wants most from me—for me to like him—is precisely what I can't give him because I don't respect him as a manager."

"You learn that you can take advantage of this manager and get away with things that you wouldn't do with another manager."

If these are the comments you're engendering through your over-Relating behaviors, you will be falling short of your main goals as a Relating manager: achieving your productivity and quality goals through having good relationships with your people. In addition, certain people will take advantage of your inherent kindness. Your need to be liked will get in the way of effective managing.

What can you do to moderate your over-Relating tendencies? Here are two ideas to make some mental shifts regarding how you manage and ten suggestions of how to actually do it.

Two Mental Shifts to Modify Over-Relating Tendencies

1. **Accept that your excessive Relating prevents you from achieving and hinders your people from growing.**

Most excessive Relaters do a good job of rationalizing their actions. They believe that their positive focus and refusal to engage in confrontation represent caring acts. But they delude themselves. Allowing someone to fail and not helping an employee grow by withholding coaching and performance information are not caring acts. An individual is responsible for his success. As a manager, you are only responsible for helping him in that endeavor. You do this by showing him what effect he is having on you and others. If you simply try to protect him from criticism or even lie to him about his performance flaws and failures, all you'll end up doing is hurting his career and encouraging him to take advantage of you. That, of course, will also hurt your career.

Becoming more Requiring and expecting more from each person is the most caring thing you can do. You must become less sensitive and concerned about making others feel bad or discussing issues where there are disagreements. Establish a relationship that endures and grows rather than trying to keep score on how the relationship is doing with every interaction. It's neither possible nor reasonable to expect that every interaction will be good.

If you're honest with your people, you're going to be telling them things that at times they don't want to hear. But in the long run, they'll respect and like you if your feedback helps them succeed. Recognize that your tendency is to focus first on how a given individual is feeling rather than if you're getting the work from him that you need. You may need to repeat the following question as a litany when you meet with your people:

> Am I really trying to help her grow and improve performance, or am I trying to make her feel good about herself so that we get along well?

The answer to this question may lead you to a small epiphany:

> The excessive aspects of your Relating behavior further *your* needs, not those of your employees.

Your people don't expect or need you to be their friend. What they expect is to be managed. They need clarity of directions and feedback, resolution of conflicts, and setting of priorities from their managers. You must become more comfortable with conflict to satisfy these expectations. Put another way, you should reconcile yourself to doing things that feel uncomfortable at first, such as telling direct reports that they need to do something differently to achieve the best outcome. None of this will happen until you understand and truly believe that your current manner is not helping you or them.

2. Add the words *long term* to statements of how you think and what you need.

The second mental shift is to think for the longer term. Over-Relaters often fall into the habit of needing respect, appreciation, and approval in almost every interaction. If a direct report is angry or even silent after an exchange, over-Relaters feel that the interaction has gone badly. Managers who attempt to solicit positive feedback from every interaction or to leave each conversation feeling good aren't being realistic. Worse, they're being bad managers.

Increase the time frame over which you ask yourself if your relationship is OK. Work toward understanding that the relationship you really want is a long-term respectful one. Every so often, imagine attending your employee's retirement dinner and envision him profusely thanking you from the podium for the help you provided throughout his career. What actions would you be taking now to earn that praise?

Clearly, they would be solely directed at helping him succeed, and any disagreements or discomfort in the process of coaching him would seem less important than they might seem now. You may not have had experiences of working through conflicts and becoming closer after they were resolved. If this is the case, you will need to trust that they can be healthy in order to be willing to experience their discomfort. Give your direct report what he needs to grow and succeed. He'll thank you for it.

Ten Action Ideas to Reduce Over-Relating

Since over-Relating is a habit used to help you meet your needs, find ways to stop the behaviors long enough to evaluate if your needs can be met without them. The following are ideas, mental games, and practices introduced in Chapter Three but here adapted to managers who need to reduce excessive Relating. Select the ideas that can work for you.

• Play "Will It Really Make a Difference?" For example, will it really make a difference if you don't spend any time today guessing what others are thinking, liking, or disliking? Try to catch yourself when this starts to happen, and stop it for a few days.

• Find a symbol or an object in your office that can be used to represent your desire to avoid being excessive in a particular activity. Whenever you look at it, it is a reminder. This is especially useful to look at before you call one of your direct reports or before you leave your office. For example, maybe a clock in your office might remind you that time is precious and you should avoid making up artificial reasons to keep in contact with your people.

• Find a phrase or mantra for the activity you are trying to reduce. Say it when you get to work, after lunch, or at other easy times to remember it. For example, maybe you need a "set priorities" mantra that you say four times when you walk into your office.

• Pretend you are a performer in a soap opera. Your role has been to be everyone's friend, reaching out to meet others' needs. This week, however, the writers are developing your character, asking you to be more observing and contemplative about *your* needs.

• Imagine that you are an impartial observer giving yourself demerits when you are over-Relating and stars when you moderate your Relating. Literally, keep track of your demerits and stars for a week.

• Look at each statement on which you rated yourself 4 on the Relating survey. Ask yourself why you do this activity "to a great extent." Are you really doing it to help another person, or does it help you feel better about yourself? How might you do this activity differently to warrant a 3?

• Create a "go-to" alternative. What might you do instead of the activity where you over-relate? Whenever you catch yourself about to over-relate, select the "go-to" alternative. Perhaps you have some activities that can be done anytime, such as some administrative paperwork. Have a file for this type of work on your desk, and use it whenever you get the urge to relate unnecessarily.

• Try a "find the obstacle" approach on the activity you want to reduce. For example, ask yourself what stops you from reducing how often you ask people how they are doing. Your obstacle might be "I'm afraid that if I don't ask, he might become unhappy and start looking for another job." In this situation, you might tell him: "I am always available to discuss your career, your satisfactions and dissatisfactions, and anything else that is on your mind. Just let me know if you want to talk." This statement might give you permission to not bring it up again, relying on him to take the responsibility to initiate a conversation.

• Play "Stretch It Out," the game where instead of doing the over-Relating activity once a day, you move it to every other day for a week, then every third day, and so on. Just by recognizing it as an over-Relating behavior, you will naturally reduce its frequency.

• Set up a complimenting system with your spouse or a friend. Agree in advance that every evening your spouse or friend will ask you if you didn't do the activity you are trying to reduce. For example, did you reduce how often you were guessing what your employees were thinking today? If the answer is yes, the other person is to compliment you. If the answer is no, the person is to say, "Well, perhaps tomorrow."

When using any of these ideas or devices, remember that your ultimate goal is to limit excessive behaviors rather than eliminate them. Asking people if they're doing OK, being empathic, empowering direct reports, and the like are all part of a good manager's job. The key principle is to take "small steps" in the right direction and keep going. Even the Great Wall of China started with a few stones set in the right direction.

ABOUT-RIGHT RELATING (7.0–8.0)

If you scored between 7.0 and 8.0 on the Relating survey and you do not identify with the excessive Relating items, you are probably Relating in the right amount. You care about your people and have established a relationship that fosters mutual respect and communication. You understand that they are responsible for their own success, but you can and do help them. You are not trying to please everyone in every interaction.

As you read about the traits of the people who under- or over-relate, if you were not about right in Relating, which one seems closer to how you manage? Look at each activity on the Relating survey for which you rated yourself a 3, and assess if you were closer to a 2 or a 4. Though you may legitimately put yourself in the "about right" category, you may tend toward one end or the other, and that information will be helpful as you combine your Relating and Requiring scores.

WHAT REQUIRERS MAY HAVE LEARNED

If you're a Requirer, you'll benefit from what you have just read in a number of ways. First, it's helpful for managers to become familiar with their less natural style. You may know some Relaters who fit the under- or over-Relating descriptions and should now have a sense of what they need to do to be more effective. To become more versatile, you need to be aware of what ideal Relating behaviors entail and what behaviors are less than ideal.

Second, did you monitor your inner voice as you were reading about over-Relating managers? Write down the specific thoughts, as they will help in Chapter Nine when you explore why you resist Relating and how you can increase your versatility.

Third, you'll find knowledge about Relating useful in dealing with both direct reports and bosses who are Relaters. Rather than dismissing Monica's seemingly absurd desire to have everyone like her, you'll recognize that she is an over-Relater who can learn to dilute this desire. If Monica works for you, you will have sufficient insight to help coach her in this direction. If Monica is your boss, you'll better understand her motivations, strengths, and weaknesses and should be able to find ways to use your strengths to complement her and help the group succeed.

Finally, the information will enable you to pinpoint whether your Relating category is low (under 7.0), about right (7.0–8.0), or high (over 8.0). The odds are that it's one of the first two.

FINDING YOUR SCORE ON THE 2R MATRIX

Requirers and Relaters now know whether their Relating and Requiring scores are low, about right, or high. Find your combination of scores in the following 2R matrix below, along with a brief characterization of your management type. In Chapter Five, I'll explain the significance of your management style and provide direction for your becoming a more effective 2R manager.

REQUIRING

		LOW	ABOUT RIGHT	HIGH
RELATING	LOW	Low Relating, Low Requiring (Abdicator)	Low Relating, About-Right Requiring (Supervisor)	Low Relating, High Requiring (Demander)
	ABOUT RIGHT	About-Right Relating, Low Requiring (Friend)	About-Right Relating, About-Right Requiring (2R Manager)	About-Right Relating, High Requiring (Energizer)
	HIGH	High Relating, Low Requiring (Pleaser)	High Relating, About-Right Requiring (Encroacher)	High Relating, High Requiring (Overwhelmer)

PART TWO

Style Familiarity

CHAPTER FIVE

Identifying Your Specific Type

～w～ Y ou've now reached the point where you can pursue a very specific course to becoming a more effective manager. You have a sense of your level of Relating and Requiring as low, about right, or high and where you fall in the 2R managerial matrix. I've given each type of manager in the grid a catchy name; take these names with a grain of salt—they're really behavioral descriptions and don't reflect the wide variation of personality styles within a given type.

REQUIRING

	LOW	ABOUT RIGHT	HIGH
LOW	Abdicator	Supervisor	Demander
ABOUT RIGHT	Friend	2R Manager	Energizer
HIGH	Pleaser	Encroacher	Overwhelmer

RELATING (left axis)

What follows is a specific characterization of these nine manager-ial types and suggestions for becoming a 2R manager. The suggestions are general at this point, outlining the directional strategy needed by each type. They will become more specific in subsequent chapters.

At first glance, it may seem naive to think that there are only nine types of managers in the world. Just as people have an infinite variety of personalities, so managers have an infinite variety of approaches. I've found, however, that these nine types are distinctly different and that all managers can find themselves close to or among these types in order to gain insight into how they manage and what actions they can take to manage better.

While you certainly should pay the most attention to your specific type, don't ignore the others. The best managers empathize with the people they work with and understand them sufficiently so that they can get the best results from them. In addition, whether you're natu-rally good at relating or requiring, understanding the types of other managers you're working with will help you become a better manager.

To that end, think about managers you know as you read the fol-lowing, and try to place them in the nine categories. As you'll discover, it's not only fun to figure out what type of manager your boss is but instructive as well.

1. THE ABDICATOR: LOW RELATING, LOW REQUIRING

If this is your type, you're an empowering, hands-off manager. You let your people do their work without much direction, follow-up, cor-rection, reshaping, or coaching. You do not define specific tasks or ob-jectives that direct reports must meet. In your own mind, you feel that you trust others and are treating them as adults. At the same time, helping your people succeed isn't a high priority for you, nor do you feel responsible for the quality of their work. You believe that it's up to them to take responsibility for what they do.

If you could view yourself through the eyes of your direct reports, however, you would have a somewhat different picture of yourself. They see your hands too far off the wheel to be driving (leading the group). They perceive you as abdicating your managerial responsibil-ity. They may believe that you don't care to spend time with them, pre-ferring to hope, trust, and avoid rather than becoming actively involved with various projects. More than once, they've wondered how you were selected to be a manager in the first place and why your bosses allow you to continue in a position in which you seem to have little interest. At the same time, they may also sense that you're someone who loves your individual contributor role. In fact, they speculate among themselves that you probably would do the organization much more good if you were assigned to an individual contributor role.

Grace is the classic abdicator. She was recently promoted to a managerial role in the corporate communications department of a pharmaceutical company. Her promotion was largely due to her outstanding contributions. Grace was a terrific public relations writer, skilled at working with the media. When one of the company's products was under intense public scrutiny because of a class action lawsuit, Grace did a stellar job of minimizing damage to the company's image by handling the press effectively. As a manager, however, Grace spends most of her time doing what she did before. She's frequently out of the office, having lunch with reporters, television producers, and the like (Grace is a journalism school graduate and former reporter). When she's in the office, she's either busy writing news releases, speeches, and letters or talking on the phone. Grace is about as hands-off a manager as anyone in her group has ever experienced. In fact, Grace has told them that she expects them to be "self-starters," that they're professionals and don't need her to hold their hands. When her people come to Grace with problems, she either brushes them off or finds an excuse for why she can't talk to them now. She also has a rule that if her door is closed, she's not to be disturbed. It's no surprise that when Grace is in the office, her door is closed more than 50 percent of the time.

How Abdicators Can Become 2R Managers

If you're like Grace, you need to become a more active manager immediately by getting closer to your people or your assignments. Even though you are low in Relating and Requiring, you have a more natural style. If it is Requiring, look at the biggest assignments you have delegated, assess how these projects are going, and talk to the individuals who are working on them. The suggestions for increasing your Requiring activities in Chapter Three should be helpful. If your natural style is Relating, spend additional time with your direct reports, asking questions and actively listening to learn what they are doing. The suggestions in Chapter Four to increase your Relating activities should help you. To become a 2R manager, you must first become a 1R manager—get one of your Rs to be about right. Relaters should relate more to move their styles closer to the "friend" type discussed next; Requirers should require more to move their styles closer to the supervisor type (discussed later in this chapter). In my experience, when Relaters see that the relationships with their people are stronger and Requirers see that they are getting more help in achieving good results, both want to continue their growth to become 2R managers.

To do this, you will need to work on developing your less natural style. This will require a major effort, as you have minimized using these skills. You may feel uncomfortable as a manager because you have little expertise or experience doing the less natural tasks your job demands. You may need to request training, take courses, and practice using the skills you acquire. Relaters should start with learning how to assert themselves more, and Requirers should start with learning how to listen better.

2. THE FRIEND: ABOUT-RIGHT RELATING, LOW REQUIRING

As a Relating manager, you care about relationships with your people. You take the initiative to ask questions, find out what individuals think, and work hard to understand others. More empathic than judgmental, you are a friend to your direct reports. Your people think of you as a nice manager who takes a sincere interest in others. You're the manager everyone likes; you may like everyone in return.

As comfortable as this role is for you, your desire to avoid conflict and keep relationships running smoothly has some negative impacts on how you manage. You are missing many opportunities to help people grow and develop. More important, you refrain from insisting on the highest-quality work. It is easier for you to be the teacher than the disciplinarian. In your quest to maintain good working relationships, you may compromise decision making, coaching, delegating, resolving conflicts, setting priorities, and dealing with poor performers quickly. You've sacrificed great performance from your people for smooth sailing.

Steve, a manager with a Silicon Valley company, would have been voted most popular manager in his organization if such things were put to a vote. He was the quintessential nice guy. People liked working for him because he communicated clearly and frequently and really listened when they had problems. However, Steve was never on the fast track and not in line for a promotion. The problem was simple: not a single person he supervised was promoted during his tenure with the company. It wasn't that his groups lacked talent but that he never did the things necessary to help people develop their talent. Steve thought he was developing people by sharing information, teaching them how to do the basics, and answering their questions. While that certainly helped them develop in one sense, it was incomplete development. He never leveled with his people about their weaknesses; he never insisted that they work to improve in certain areas. Steve's new boss was a firm believer in developing talent in-house rather than recruiting stars, and Steve's reputation as a good guy didn't compensate for his poor record as a developer of people.

How Friends Can Become 2R Managers

If your managerial style is that of a friend, your obstacle is your desire to befriend your people rather than help them grow or make some waves in the pursuit of doing great work. What you need to accept is that your relationship will weaken as time goes by unless you help your people more and insist on higher-quality work being done. You will have to endure some short-term relationship discomfort in order to have a very strong long-term relationship. By being more direct and more demanding than feels comfortable, you can earn their gratitude and respect as their manager. Your people will feel better if they are urged to do better work. They will eventually thank you for whatever push you give them toward advancing their careers.

The versatility you need can be achieved if you work on your requiring skills. Start by accepting that your current managerial style fails to help your people achieve their potential and doesn't allow the group as a whole to produce the highest-quality work. Next think about why you resist being more Requiring. Why is it so important that everyone like you? Why are you afraid of people resenting what you tell them or even becoming angry with you? Once you come to terms with your concerns about becoming more Requiring, you have to commit to asserting yourself (saying directly what you really want to say without worrying so much about the impact). This activity will put you in a discomfort zone, but this is necessary to achieve change. Asserting is a good interim step; it's not as big a style jump as pure Requiring. Once you become more comfortable with it, Requiring is only one step further. In addition, managers who practice being assertive often don't have to make the leap to Requiring behaviors. Their assertiveness often suffices, giving them access to a behavioral option they previously lacked.

3. THE PLEASER: HIGH RELATING, LOW REQUIRING

Even more than the friend, you care tremendously about relationships with your people. As a strong Relater, you ask questions, find out what direct reports think and feel, and work hard to understand them. Your empathy and your ability to know your direct reports personally are strong points, but they're negated by your obsession with pleasing them. As much as you like people and they like you, managing makes you uncomfortable because there are so many activities that can put relationships in jeopardy by displeasing people.

Everything revolves around your need to establish good relationships with your direct reports. By attempting to please people during every interaction, you fail to realize that this behavior may end up not pleasing them in the long run (you don't give them the sort of consistent, honest feedback that will help them grow in their careers). Because you bend over backward to avoid conflict and fail to level with them, your group doesn't produce much high-quality work. To keep relationships in good shape, you compromise decision making, coaching, and developing others, asking for work to be redone until it is excellent, resolving conflicts, setting priorities, delegating, and dealing with poor performers quickly. You are neither getting the best from your people nor giving them the best, even though your intentions are good.

It's easy for pleasers like Linda to rationalize their behavior. A thirty-eight-year-old manager of a corporate library, Linda is certain that she's a better manager than others in her company because she really cares about her people. She's convinced herself that if she just provides her direct reports with sufficient emotional support, resources, and freedom, they will shine. It's true that one person in Linda's group does shine, but the other five do not. Two of them get away with murder, recognizing that Linda values her relationship with them more than she values their work. As a result, they're frequently too casual in responding to urgent requests and not disciplined to be thorough. Linda knows she is not getting good work from them, but she doesn't know how to correct the situation. When Linda's boss confronts her about her reports' spotty work, she immediately comes to her people's defense, insisting that they're "good guys" who just have bad days like everyone else.

How Pleasers Can Become 2R Managers

As a pleaser, your need to be liked verges on the obsessive; it's not just a moderate, natural impulse, as it is for the friend. If you don't work on reducing this need, you are unlikely to improve as a manager. All management activities raise conflicts, putting you in a difficult spot. What might open your eyes is that the thing you want most—a close relationship with people—is not what you're going to get if you continue to be a pleaser. Though it may seem like your people want you to keep them happy, what they also want is for you to help them develop and grow. They need you to manage them.

You need to implement the ideas for reducing your over-Relating tendencies, as described in Chapter Four, to get your most natural R closer to about right. Focus on converting your need to be liked into the need to be respected over the long term. If you can do this, you'll find that you can reduce your over-Relating and start behaving assertively without being terrified that it will hurt your relationships. Once your Relating is about right, you can redirect more and more energy to asserting yourself in order to improve the quality of work coming from your group. The process of becoming more versatile may be a slow one, as you have to overcome your natural resistance to conflict and confrontations. You will need to make a major commitment to your personal development to acquire your second R.

4. THE SUPERVISOR: LOW RELATING, ABOUT-RIGHT REQUIRING

As a manager who focuses on results and achievements, you're able to crank out good work consistently. You know what you want and are clear in asking for it. Your ability to set priorities, resolve issues, and keep your eye on the ball translates into results. When you interact with your people, the interaction usually revolves around the task; you're not as comfortable in non-task-oriented people situations. Spending your time efficiently is very important to you. Overall, you feel comfortable with your style and are reluctant to change.

If you could eavesdrop on your direct reports, however, you might be more willing to make some changes. You're viewed as a no-nonsense boss who uses people rather than builds teams. Because your attitude and actions discourage others from talking to you about anything beyond the routine, they are reluctant to approach you with new ideas or suggestions for improvements. Part of the problem is that people don't feel you appreciate or understand them as individuals. Your responses to people are all the same, not based on their particular needs or interests. You may treat them fairly, but you don't treat them with much compassion, warmth, or individuality. You are willing to show them what to do but aren't eager to coach them to reach their potential. Though you're not aware of it, you're missing opportunities to increase your group's results. You don't realize that your best people—the ones who are ambitious and determined to grow—won't stay with you because you're not facilitating that growth. You'll be left with people who are comfortable being told what to do. It's likely that you're not overly concerned about your current situation since you're not having a big negative impact. At the same time, you may sense that your managerial contribution is limited and that you could have a much greater positive impact.

Denise is a classic supervisor. Her engineering company has promoted her a number of times because management prizes her efficiency. Denise always meets her deadlines and rarely messes up a project. While her extreme competency met the needs of her higher-ups early on, they've been disappointed in her group's performance recently. Given more important projects where personal competency isn't enough, she's been unable to motivate her team to put in the time and come up with the breakthrough ideas that are deemed critical. Her group lacks creativity. Denise's boss assumed she would rise to the challenge, but she seems capable of only getting jobs done right; she can't push her group's performance to the next level. This frustrates her, because she places a high value on results, but telling people exactly what to do doesn't seem to be the solution.

How Supervisors Can Become 2R Managers

As a supervisor, your path to improvement resides in your strength. You relish accomplishing tasks, and you probably realize that if you motivated other people to become more involved in these tasks, you'd be able to accomplish more. In other words, you must master the art of creating a real team working toward goals. This will multiply your contribution. But you can't do this unless you overcome your resistance to Relating.

Listening and encouraging others are the two main skills of Relating, and these are the skills you should attempt to acquire. Given your low Relating score, you should start out with the short-term strategy of just making a conscious effort to encourage and listen more. Give yourself a task to understand what your direct reports are meaning when they talk to you. Ask enough questions, and resist judging in order to hear them better. You may not be great at these skills initially, but you don't have to be. Over the short term, practicing these skills is the key. Over the long term, you will want to be good at these skills, but don't beat yourself up if you feel awkward when you encourage a direct report or if you find yourself not paying as much attention as you should when someone else is talking. Practice and commitment will enable most supervisor managers to improve these skills.

5. THE 2R MANAGER: ABOUT-RIGHT RELATING, ABOUT-RIGHT REQUIRING

You are in prime 2R territory, generally doing the right things and doing them in the right amount. You reach out to establish relationships with each of your people, and you hold them accountable for the work you assign. Whether it's asking questions to assess their progress or insisting on levels of performance, you can do both when needed. You treat each person who works for you as an individual, and you have created a cooperative environment where people collaborate and participate. Confident in yourself and others, you enjoy both the people and task sides of your job. Since you regularly practice both Relating and Requiring behaviors, you're probably a very good manager.

Alice, thirty-five, has been promoted three times since she joined a Fortune 100 company right after receiving her M.B.A. A natural 2R manager—she was one of those rare individuals who scored "about right" in both Rs almost from the start of her career—Alice thrived in each successive managerial position. When she had to be tough and hold her people's feet to the fire, she was able to do so. In her first position, Alice inherited a team that was complacent and even a bit lazy. Alice demanded accountability from each person and was not afraid of asserting her authority, even though some team members were older and more experienced than she was. At the same time, Alice's communication skills were so well developed that she listened when people told her she was placing unreasonable demands on them. Though she didn't always agree with their feedback, she welcomed and responded to it, making her people feel that she valued their contributions. It should come as no surprise that the executives at the company view Alice as an excellent prospect for a future top-management position.

How 2R Managers Can Become *Better* 2R Managers

To become a better 2R manager, you can use the following strategies:

• Increase your depth of understanding of others. Read about each type of manager as carefully as you read about 2R managers. Think of managers you know of each type, and consider what they need to do to increase their effectiveness. By becoming sensitive to other types and their needs, you will learn how to help your people achieve their goals.

• Be aware of your own leanings. If you weren't a 2R manager, what would you be? In which direction would your tests have tended? Study the section of the specific type you most closely resemble, and determine in what kinds of situations you behave like this type. By recognizing your tendencies, you can do a better job of maintaining your about-right approaches to Requiring and Relating.

• Increase your Relating and Requiring skills. Chapters Eight and Nine should help 2R managers with ideas for improving their Relating and Requiring skills. Though you're comfortable using both, you probably have room for improvement in each.

• Become more savvy about when to relate and when to require. Although you possess versatility, you may not always use it effectively. Recognizing that you always have the option of using the other R, analyze which one will work best for each situation. Chapter Ten will help you here.

6. THE ENCROACHER: HIGH RELATING, ABOUT-RIGHT REQUIRING

You are a dynamic, energetic manager who relates easily and achieves a lot. It is easier for you to take the initiative to relate than to require, but you can do both. If your test scores were very close, you may have had some difficulty in Chapter Two figuring out if you were a Relater or a Requirer, as you identify with only a few of the excessive characteristics of high Relaters. Similarly, in Chapter Four, you probably identified with the need to be liked and the high sensitivity to others' reactions, but not necessarily to the fear or avoidance of asserting your views and needs.

On the plus side, you work very comfortably with your people and are unafraid to ask for what you want. You are often thinking about how to help them and what they should know to do their jobs well. You share your views, feelings, and goals easily. When your employees want to talk, you can listen with empathy and understanding. You have clear goals and a strong desire to achieve them.

Your style results from a mixture of two powerful needs: the need to be liked and the need to achieve. You enjoy doing both at the same time—relating to people and having fun as you accomplish goals together. When you work with your people, the relating usually has priority; you are comfortable taking more time than is absolutely necessary for the task. If the task is urgent, however, you can focus all your energy on it. One of the important things to note is that you control which mode of operating you and your people are in—the urgent task mode or the more Relating, enjoyable, working-together-to-get-it-done mode.

As the name "encroacher" suggests, however, you sometimes cross the line and violate a direct report's privacy. You fail to observe necessary boundaries. For instance, you may feel free to enter your people's offices at any time. Your agenda (which often includes helping your people even when they aren't asking for the help) is strong, and you pursue it assertively. You may not be aware of how controlling you can be of your people's time. You get results, but you may not get them in ways your people appreciate, and that can undermine future cooperation. For instance, though you may project the image of a nice guy by Relating to get what you want, you're not averse to pushing hard if that isn't working. Your employees may feel that you deceived them with your nice-guy persona and that the only thing that counts for you is getting your way. They end up feeling maneuvered or manipulated, which raises their resistance to giving you what you want.

Dave manages a team of four people at a medium-sized advertising agency. He makes it a practice of taking his people out to lunch, dropping in for "chats," and even calling them at home at night and on weekends to discuss work issues. Although the people in Dave's group think he's generally a good boss and fun to work with, they resent the way he uses his frequent interactions to "check up on them."

One of his people noted that the two of them might be talking about their golf games one minute and the next Dave's back to probing about a project they discussed earlier in the day. It feels intrusive, as if every thought, discussion, or idea has to be shared with him. Dave's group works hard and delivers results, but its members are working below their potential because they don't trust him enough to be honest with him. If they were more open with Dave and willing to share their ideas, they could probably resolve problems and finish assignments faster.

How Encroachers Can Become 2R Managers

As an encroacher, you have a great opportunity to do *less* and accomplish *more*. Being less controlling will work wonders, allowing your people more "space" in which to function on their own. If you can back off a bit, it will be easier to earn your direct reports' trust. Encroachers who realize they don't have to over-relate to get what they want generally become more effective managers.

To moderate these tendencies, be alert for signs that your people are trying to tell you to give them more room. Specifically, recognize that you're encroaching when your direct reports fail to return your phone calls promptly (or at all), come up with polite excuses to avoid you, become distracted or drift off when you're talking to them, fail to reach out to talk to you about important issues, or seem to resist your friendliness. If you use your sensitivity to spot these instances, you will learn when you need to give your direct reports more autonomy.

Although encroachers' test scores are about right for the Requiring functions, it is my experience that while they think about Requiring correctly—they know they should insist on high quality and ask people to redo their work—their implementation is often less effective. If the encroacher hasn't gotten what she wants, her Requiring or asserting words often have unintended effects. She may show her disappointment or frustration. Or she may be rude or insulting and not know it. Therefore, encroachers can gain from reviewing and refining their asserting and Requiring skills.

7. THE DEMANDER: LOW RELATING, HIGH REQUIRING

You are a Requiring manager who cares tremendously about getting results and achieving great things. You know what you want and are clear in asking for it. As a result, you're good at getting work out on time, setting priorities, resolving issues, and delivering what you promise. Your energy and sense of urgency help you accomplish a great deal. Although you may encounter a significant amount of resistance from your people in response to your demands, you aren't bothered by it and move forward relentlessly.

Your people, however, are bothered. Viewing you as a one-dimensional boss, they may be alienated by the combination of your demanding nature and your unwillingness to give much empathy and communication in return. You have lost your share of good people who resent your inability to show appreciation for their contributions. You are constantly telling people what to do, assuming that they are incapable of doing things without continuous, explicit instructions. In response, your people stop showing initiative and wait for you to tell them what to do. You miss out on good ideas because you don't foster participative decision making. As quick as you are to criticize, you're slow to praise.

Inflexible is the word Larry's people use to describe him. Larry, however, defines his rigidity as "an unwavering demand for the highest quality." He is convinced that the only way to achieve this goal is by telling his people exactly how to do each job. *Compromise* is not in his vocabulary. If he lets up even a little, Larry believes, people will take advantage of what they perceive as his "weakness." For this reason, Larry refused to allow Darlene to make a presentation to his boss. Even though Darlene was the most talented and hardest-working member of his group and had done all the research on the new product introduction, Larry adamantly rejected her request to be the presenter. Larry believed that Darlene would somehow "mess up" the presentation, that he couldn't control everything she said to his boss, and that she would create problems. Larry did the presentation while Darlene listened, and it went smoothly. Two months later, however, Darlene quit. It wasn't only that Larry took over the presentation but that Larry was always the sole arbiter of quality. He wasn't open to letting anyone else contribute. She was tired of feeling unappreciated and underutilized.

How Demanders Can Become 2R Managers

As a demander, your focus on getting things done the way you want them done is excessive; it's not just a moderate, natural impulse, as it is for a supervisor type. You are always ready to pounce—to correct, direct, insist, and demand. The speed at which you exhibit these be-haviors shows that you assume your employees will not get it right. It doesn't take long before they don't do much on their own, looking to you for instructions on how you want it. This builds a dependence that you may like but does not get the best performance from your people. And your best people will not take it very long. You need to trust some people more and lighten up on the controls. You need to imple-ment the ideas of Chapter Three to reduce your strong over-Requiring tendencies. Just as important, you must learn why you resist the Re-lating activities that would help you get the best from your people. When you can let go of that resistance as you are letting go of some of the controls, you will see that you have access to new ways to get-ting what you want. The key skills you must learn are to become a bet-ter listener and encourager. You will need to make a major commitment to acquire your second R.

8. THE ENERGIZER: ABOUT-RIGHT RELATING, HIGH REQUIRING

The energizer is a results-oriented manager who, unlike the deman-der, knows how to listen and encourage. You enjoy people, relate with ease, and have a powerful drive to achieve and succeed. Your strong sense of mission causes you to push yourself, others in your group, and probably your managers, too. Setting priorities, resolving con-flicts, and giving directions come naturally as you lead your team. You have ambitious dreams of what you can achieve and every expecta-tion of realizing them.

With the speed and strength you exhibit, you can undermine your direct reports' efforts to help you. While you can listen to and en-courage your direct reports, you often feel you know what they are going to say and don't let them finish. You may not show enough pa-tience if they process information slowly, or you may dismiss new in-formation too quickly. More important, using words that emerge naturally from your strong Requiring nature, you can come across a lot rougher than you mean to be. You probably don't realize that you intimidate some of your people or that your high-energy approach can be overwhelming. In some circumstances, what you view as Re-lating, others view as challenging, probing, judging, or manipulating.

Julia, for instance, always seems to be "turned on". She usually talks loudly and intensely and is tremendously enthusiastic about her proj-ects. Julia has such strong goals and ambitions for the group, she dominates most conversations, finishes others' sentences, and is always eager to describe the way an individual or the group should proceed. What Julia doesn't realize is that she startles people—her energy precludes their participation. They would like to be heard, too. Most of the members of her team are young, and though they don't tell her this, they feel as if they're never going to be able to match her work ethic or her animated approach to the job.

How Energizers Can Become 2R Managers

Most energizers pride themselves on their high-revving engines and recognize that their bosses value the enthusiasm and aggressiveness they bring to their jobs. The key to becoming a better manager, however, is recognizing that this energy is having some unintended consequences and taking the necessary steps to change. Pay attention to the reaction of your people when you start shooting off sparks. You have the charm and Relating skills to slow down, lighten up, and listen better. Recognize that for some direct reports, your intensity is intimidating, and that if you reduce it, you'll find that they're much more responsive to what you're asking them to do. These adaptations in your style can bring you toward 2R managing and a much higher probability of achieving your ambitions.

9. THE OVERWHELMER: HIGH RELATING, HIGH REQUIRING

This is a highly unusual type. While high Relating and high Requiring aren't mutually exclusive states, they are infrequently seen in the same individual. Therefore, you need to make sure you really belong in this category. In fact, you probably operate more like an energizer or an encroacher than you do an overwhelmer. Redo the tests in the earlier chapters, asking yourself if you're answering the questions from the standpoint of what you actually do and not what you feel you should be doing.

• Did you answer that you are "to a great extent" available to listen, collaborate, coach, teach, and help with a problem in the Relating survey while also answering that you are "to a great extent" very efficient in the use of your time and communicate the importance of meeting deadlines?

- Are you "to a great extent" wanting people to like you, friendly, eager to change something if a direct report is overworked, while simultaneously "to a great extent" insisting on the highest quality, controlling projects and assignments, and expecting people to do whatever it takes to complete every request?
- Are you "to a great extent" both individually competitive and highly cooperative?

You can probably sense from these questions my skepticism about whether you belong in this category. If you're convinced that this type fits you, however, get some input from your employees by asking them to complete the twelve-question test in "More Resources for the 2R Manager" at the back of the book. The results should help you determine if you are, indeed, an overwhelmer.

If you are a confirmed overwhelmer, you may well be an outstanding individual achiever, and your extreme style may have earned you a coterie of followers. You have skills in both Relating and Requiring, but you're squandering that talent because you're not managing people effectively.

Like an encroacher, you cross boundaries with your over-Relating behaviors. Like a demander, you press people to the point of breaking in order to get work done. The combination of your high-energy demands and your need to control through constant communication smothers your direct reports. As a result, they rarely, if ever, shine or feel good about their work; their development is stunted by the way in which you overdo all your managerial behaviors.

William, who works for an international management consulting firm, is a true overwhelmer. The best business developer at the firm, he listens carefully to prospects and responds with brilliant proposals that seem as if he's read prospects' minds. Charming and able to achieve instant rapport with clients, William seemed as if he would shine when he was promoted to the top new business development position at the firm. Unfortunately, he has failed miserably, primarily because he has been unable to develop the talent of the people on his team. Reflexively deferring to his suggestions, they never learn to master the gamut of skills necessary to be a great new business developer. Typically, the best people work for William for about a year and then, wanting more freedom to grow, either request a transfer or leave the company. Not only have new business efforts fallen off at the firm, but it has lost some of the best young talent it had.

How Overwhelmers Can Become 2R Managers

If you're an overwhelmer, you can take heart in the adage "With age comes wisdom." You often self-correct at least some of your excessive behaviors as you learn from experience. Over time, you realize you're smothering people—perhaps you've received some feedback to this effect over the years—and you naturally back off. Delegating more tasks, taking less initiative, and relinquishing the need for tight control are some positive actions you can take. As you become older and wiser, you may lean toward wanting to leave a legacy and then become less concerned with personal achievement; you may become interested in seeing your people do well, deriving satisfaction from contributing to their success.

You can't change how old or experienced you are, but you can be open to learning from your experiences. Try to develop a perspective about your role as a manager, and recognize that there is more than one way to manage. Be open to feedback and willing to adapt, based on what you hear. You may also want to review the advice for encroachers and energizers, since it's frequently applicable to overwhelmers as well.

As you went through Chapters Three and Four, your test scores show that you were both an over-Requirer and an over-Relater. The advice given to reduce excessive Requiring in Chapter Three should be completely applicable to you, as you will need to lighten up and reduce your intensity. The advice given to reduce excessive Relating in Chapter Four may or may not apply, as you are not shy to assert yourself or require of others, as is the case with other over-Relaters. You will need to evaluate how you exhibit your need to be liked and whether those behaviors are serving their purpose.

USING YOUR OPPOSITE TYPE TO LEARN ABOUT YOURSELF

The more you know about your particular managerial type—the more you understand about your particular mix of Relating and Requiring tendencies—the more successfully you'll move toward the 2R ideal. The following are three sets of opposite but matched types that should help you gain insights into your particular managerial behaviors and how you might change them.

The Demander and the Pleaser

The demander is too high in Requiring and too low in Relating; the pleaser is just the opposite. Both overuse their natural style and become a 1R manager, relying on their strong R so much that it ceases to be effective. Both need to make major changes. This won't happen until they recognize that they're not accomplishing what they care about most. The pleaser is not really pleasing or helping employees, and the demander is not getting the work done well enough through others. In most cases, their people want out.

The pleaser's direct reports know they are in control of the relationship, as the manager is trying too hard to please them. Poor and marginal performers can take advantage of this manager, and good performers want the manager to coach more, make more decisions, and move the group ahead. The demander's direct reports aren't participating; they don't feel valued or part of a team. Therefore, they resist their manager's demands. Poor performers don't last long, and good performers want a different manager who will appreciate their contribution.

Of the two corrective actions needed, reducing overreliance on the natural style and learning to use the less natural style, the latter is more difficult due to the lack of practice and reward. Using one's less natural style conflicts with habit and belief. For both demanders and pleasers, the differential between the Requiring scores and Relating scores is great. As a result, they feel that any move to increase use of the less natural style will result in becoming like their opposite, which they view as unacceptable. When a pleaser tries to require, he feels like the demander, whom he dislikes and does not want to become. Likewise, the demander avoids any move that will make her feel like a pleaser.

To overcome these obstacles, both need to realize that nothing they do will make them even remotely like their opposite type. For example, Ian is a demander who has just started to understand he must try to relate more. He decides he is going to ask his employees more about themselves and their feelings about work. Monday morning, he goes to Jane and asks, "How's it going?" He feels he has just acted like a Relater, not knowing that his tone conveys, "You've got five seconds to answer, or my interest is gone." Ian fears he's becoming a pleaser, not knowing that the pleaser, using the same words, would convey, "I'm available to listen to your life story, including the birth of each of your children."

Conversely, Sue is a pleaser. She has a high need to be liked, but she has just started to understand she must demand more of her employees. One of her direct reports, Mark, a chronic late arriver, is clearly taking advantage of her good nature. Monday morning, Sue decides she will take this issue on. She goes to Mark and says, "Mark, we are all part of a team here. Could you please come to work on time?" Her tone, however, communicates that she is *asking* Mark if it is OK with him to arrive on time. Mark is smart enough to say yes. Sue thinks she is Requiring, but the tone gives her away. She is never going to act like the over-Requiring person who is her worst nightmare.

What feels like giant leaps are really baby steps in learning to be more versatile. Remembering this truism makes these small steps easier.

The Friend and the Supervisor

Both friends and supervisors use their more natural style about right and are low in the less natural style. By not using the less natural style, however, both have one hand tied behind their back. As a result, solvable problems remain unsolved. For instance, a supervisor may keep trying to tell a direct report how to perform better when all he needs is someone to complain to about his problems; just getting an issue off his chest will restore his enthusiasm and energy. Unable to lend him an empathic ear, the supervisor leaves him stuck in his unproductive rut.

Supervisors need to learn to be more like friends and friends to be more like supervisors. Both types of managers resist being like the other but would gain from developing skills the other possesses.

The friend has problems with poor or marginal employees who take advantage of her desire to avoid conflict. She has difficulty telling an employee what she wants or needs done. The friend may tolerate marginal performance far too long, negatively affecting the morale of her team and its best people. She may have some decision-making problems if many conflicts are involved. The activities she avoids almost always relate to conflict, confrontation, and feeling OK about her authority as a manager.

While the supervisor has all these issues mastered, he experiences problems with good employees who are not growing as individuals. He is not a great listener; why should he listen to others when he knows how to do the job and enjoys doing it his way? Good people want to leave after they have learned what they can from him. His lack of closeness with his people deprives him of their best ideas, and he's not particularly interested in or adept at creating teams. The friend, of course, is skilled at all these activities. Increasing your versatility, therefore, begins with observing the skills of your opposite counterpart's style.

The Encroacher and the Energizer

Both encroachers and energizers are high-energy, results-oriented managers. The encroacher relies on Relating to get employees to do what she wants, while the energizer depends on Requiring skills, but both will use their less natural style when necessary. Here the more natural style is being overused and the less natural style is used about the right amount. It is my experience that while the energizer can relate and the encroacher can require, these less natural skills are often carried out with some unintended consequences. For example, the energizer may sound impatient or accusatory when he feels he is asking questions and listening (Relating). The encroacher may sound disappointed or pouty when she feels she is stating what she wants (Requiring). The result is that direct reports of both manager types do not completely trust their managers and may view them as manipulating or controlling.

Both types must learn to relate more effectively, by becoming more sensitive to negative impacts of their respective behaviors. The energizer risks losing trust and input as his people become resistant or closed off when pushed too hard. He must learn to lighten up but also relate legitimately, giving Relating the time it deserves and without having a Requiring agenda. The encroacher risks include losing trust and violating her employees' need for privacy. She must learn when to reduce her Relating behaviors and to require in ways that don't undermine her previous Relating actions. These adjustments are not huge ones, but they are important.

Encroachers and energizers both have enormous potential to excel and become 2R managers. They both need to lighten up their natural behaviors while legitimizing their less natural behaviors.

From the foregoing analyses, you may have a good idea what direction you need to take to become a 2R manager. The problem is translating that idea into action. As we'll see, many managers are stuck in the rut of their primary R.

CHAPTER SIX

Getting Unstuck

M ost managers favor one R over the other. Even abdicators, 2R managers, and overwhelmers have a more natural R. Nonetheless, you may feel you can use willpower to stop favoring your natural R as much as you did in the past. Unfortunately, as with eating less or getting more exercise, most of us need more than willpower to escape long-entrenched behavioral patterns. Though we understand completely what we *should* do based on a particular profile, we find ourselves being pulled inexorably back despite our best intentions to change.

Typically, some managers respond to their profiled types by being highly conscious of managerial behaviors; for a while, they stop over-relying on Relating or Requiring actions and start using the other R more. Over time, however, they become less conscious about their behaviors and gradually revert to type. Other managers can't even make temporary changes. They know what their type is and the associated strengths and weaknesses, but they just can't desert their dominant managerial style. They are comfortable handling the reactions they generate from their current approach. Consciously or not, they believe their success is based largely on how they've used their dominant

R in the past. They fear that if they break from that style, they will endanger their effectiveness and their careers.

If we think of being restricted to one managerial style as being locked up, finding the key to greater freedom of behavior is crucial. There are a number of things you can do to decrease the hold your natural style has on your managerial attitudes and actions. Let's start with Requirers.

THE KEY TO UNLOCKING REQUIRERS

To unlock a reliance on Requiring, we need to look closely at exactly what Requirers do:

QUESTION: What does a Requirer do when he isn't getting what he wants from his employees?

MOST COMMON ANSWER: He tries to be clearer about what he wants, spelling out his request in greater detail. If clarification doesn't work, he may be overtly critical to the employee. If criticism doesn't work, he will ultimately either take over the project himself or give it to someone else.

Many Requirers can't escape from the cycle of clarifying, criticizing, and usurping. No matter how many times they swear they're not going to fall into the same energy-draining, time-consuming trap, they do anyway.

If you find yourself in this cycle, you need to understand it more. Once you are aware of why you respond in a specific Requiring manner, you will find it easier to shift the pattern. To that end, imagine that you're the manager in the following scenario.

You head a group of strategy consultants and have asked Ed, one of your staff members, to look into how a utilities company (one of your clients) might expand into a new line of service. You assign Ed to conduct research, write a summary report, and prepare the client presentation. Two days before the client meeting, you review Ed's work. As you're reading, you become increasingly agitated. His report is wordy and technical, failing to highlight key points or narrow the alternatives. While you recognize that some good research and strong ideas have gone into the report, you know it won't meet the client's needs. You're anxious about the client and the meeting, and you know what type of report will help this client expand into a new business area.

At this point, what would you do?

(a) Take the project over yourself, whipping the report into shape.

(b) Clarify again what you want Ed to do and let him do it.

If you're a strong Requirer, you'll probably decide to do the report yourself. If you're a demander, for instance, you probably won't care that you're robbing Ed of a valuable development experience by usurping his responsibility. On the other hand, if you're an energizer, you may choose to clarify the project for Ed and let him take another crack at it. If he doesn't make much of an improvement on his second draft, however, your quality-control impulse will go into overdrive, and you'll probably do the report yourself.

Let's assume for the sake of this scenario that Ed is a bright, talented employee who is worth coaching. You want Ed to learn from this experience. Stop for a minute and ask yourself how you would coach Ed. Try to decide what you would really do, as opposed to what you think you should do. Did you select any of the following?

(a) Use the report you wrote as a teaching tool, reviewing it with Ed and telling him that this is the type of work you expect from him on the next project.

(b) Explain why Ed's report was inadequate, pointing out that clients respond poorly to the level of technical detail he included in his report, the lack of a few solid alternatives, and so on.

(c) Give Ed a motivational talk designed to let him know that he let you down and you expect him to perform better next time.

(d) Decide that next time you give Ed an assignment, you must be much clearer with him about how he should create a report.

As a Requirer, you probably had one or more of these reactions. Unfortunately, all four reactions involve "telling." Requirers usually try to teach, explain, motivate, and clarify in order to get the performance they want from their people. In many cases, telling might work. But Ed already resisted this telling approach, and you found it difficult to try something different.

Having used the Ed scenario with hundreds of Requiring managers, I've found that almost none of them considers asking him, "Why do you feel the need to include so much technical detail in your client report?" Asking a question, rather than telling, is a Relating skill, and a Requirer might deem it irrelevant—what does it matter why Ed chose to present the report the way he did? The answer lies in the possibility of your learning something that will help you manage Ed better. You might learn that to Ed, quality is synonymous with thoroughness. If he weren't thorough, he wouldn't feel he did a good job. His value system places this attentiveness to detail above everything else, and nothing you can tell him—no matter how "clear" or motivational you might be—is going to change his priorities. A sound Relating approach, on the other hand, would allow you to find a solution that both serves the client and recognizes Ed's value system. You might say, "Why don't you prepare a detailed report to give to the client, but let's agree on the main points and the way in which we will summarize them." Acknowledging Ed's values and building consensus with him will not only result in a good report but also help him learn that he needs to adjust his needs and approaches to match the clients' needs in the future. Before examining how you can escape your reflexive requiring response to this type of situation, let's look at another scenario.

Anita is a wonderful worker. She is bright, writes well, and thinks creatively. She has been with you for just over a year now, mostly doing research or analysis behind the scenes. You feel she is ready to do more, and you ask her to manage a project with people from different departments. To your surprise, Anita responds with uncertainty; she expresses doubt that she is ready for such an assignment. You had expected her to be excited that you were giving her this opportunity, and instead she seems almost upset that you're asking her to manage the project.

What might you do to help Anita in this situation?

When this problem was posed to a group of Requirers, some of the answers included communicating the following to Anita:

"I know you can do it."

"I wouldn't have given you this assignment if I didn't think you could do it."

"You're smart; you can handle it."

"Just get started on it; it will flow from there."

In a Requiring manager's mind, these responses all make sense. Unfortunately, they fall into the tell, teach, explain, clarify, or motivate mode again. Anita suffers from a lack of confidence, and simply telling her that *you* believe she is capable won't make *her* believe it. Is there a different approach that might prevent her lack of self-confidence from undermining her efforts?

By now, you know to ask her why she is not sure she can do it. That process might give you more information to help her. She may answer that she's not sure about one aspect of the project, and you may be able to provide her with certain resources that will assuage her fears. But what if, after hearing Anita tell you why she lacks confidence in her ability and you've offered assistance, Anita says, "I don't know. I'm just not sure I'm ready"? Now what?

At this point, a typical Requirer might become annoyed with Anita for her lack of confidence—for not being more like you. You might repeat how simple the job is or explain the assignment again, reverting to your more natural words. What you have to get beyond is your conviction that Anita can handle the project if you just give her a little push. Yes, she has the talent and experience to manage the project. Yes, you think she's great. But that isn't enough. She is not going to reach her potential if she continues to harbor so much self-doubt, and you aren't addressing the issue correctly by telling her she shouldn't feel this way.

Specifically, you need to employ the Relating skills of nurturing and encouraging. This means consistently and interactively proving to Anita that her talents are up to the task. She doesn't just need one compliment but many, delivered in a variety of ways. You need to listen to her anxieties, and no matter how trivial or silly they seem, take them seriously. She needs to know that you're listening. Sometimes, articulating fears helps diminish their intensity. Sometimes, however, the people you manage will need you to nurture them in other ways. You may have to give her a smaller assignment as an interim step to prove that she can handle a bigger project. You may have to offer frequent verbal support before she feels ready to take on a major assignment.

You might ask Anita what is the worst-case scenario after she expresses her self-doubt, going light on the word *worst* to avoid showing impatience. If you ask with a sincere interest in the answer, she may respond that she is afraid of failing, of letting you, the group, and the organization down. In response to this or some other fear, ask her, "Is this outcome likely, given how you've performed before when working on challenging assignments?"

Because Anita is talented and works hard, she has probably succeeded at increasingly difficult assignments in the past. Reminded of these accomplishments, she will feel a bit more confident—you're providing her with tangible evidence that she can be effective when the degree of difficulty increases. You may also need to reassure her that if there's something she doesn't know that's important for the new assignment, she will learn it. Again, you may have to refer to her history of successfully learning new skills and handling new assignments. Finally, you may need to remind her, gently, that she doesn't have to be perfect, that mistakes are part of learning, that she shouldn't feel she has to complete the new project without a single misstep, and that no one expects her to get everything right the first time.

This is going to be difficult for you. Requirers are naturally impatient and instinctively feel that nurturing and encouraging wastes valuable time. The short-term time expenditure, however, will be more than redeemed by the long-term increase in your direct reports' productivity and development. Remember that developing the potential of talented people is just as important as getting results immediately.

To give yourself these relating options and prevent your requiring instinct from dominating your managerial behaviors, try to think about the following two points:

• If what you're doing isn't working, you need to try a different approach. When your direct reports aren't responding positively to your managerial approach, remind yourself that you can't always *tell, explain, or clarify* how others need to do their work. As a Requirer, you are a practical problem solver. You need more information to do your best work and solve the problem of how to work best with each employee. Develop the ability to identify early when you are trying too hard to solve a people-related problem with your natural approach and consciously say, "I may need to try the Monty Python approach: 'And now for something completely different.'"

• Relating enhances the effectiveness of your Requiring activities. For example, if you do not listen to your people or show interest in their issues and problems, over time they will not listen to you any more than they absolutely have to. On the other hand, if you listen to your people and respect their concerns, they will want to give you more of what you want.

The most effective and quickest route for you to relate better (and solve people-related roadblocks) is through asking and listening (to learn more) or through encouraging and nurturing (to support more). Chapter Nine is devoted entirely to helping you develop these skills.

THE KEY TO UNLOCKING RELATERS

To unlock a reliance on Relating, we need to look closely at exactly what Relaters do.

QUESTION: What does a Relater do when she is not getting what she wants from her employee?

MOST COMMON ANSWER: Because she often concludes that it may be her fault for not spending enough time to develop a better relationship with the employee, her first response is to spend more time Relating. If this doesn't work, she drops hints about what she wants him to do and hopes he picks up on it.

As a Relater, you don't want to feel like a bad guy by demanding too much of your people. You're locked in to your particular R because of your compassion and desire to please others. Without your empathy and your ability to connect with your people, you would not have built such strong relationships in the past. While you may intellectually recognize that you rely too heavily on your Relating skills, you may not realize how much you are psychologically dependent on them. To understand how this is so, put yourself in the following scenario.

You have been very understanding of Colleen, who needs a lot of flexibility due to her responsibilities as a single mom. A few times when you really needed her help, however, she was unavailable, and her excuses sounded weak. In the latest situation, after receiving a request from your boss for a quick analysis of a problem in your division, you asked Colleen to work on it, noting that there had to be a quick turnaround. She said she couldn't do it because she promised to take her son shopping for clothes, and she needed to leave work a little early. As a result of Colleen's declining the project, you put off your other work and spent all afternoon addressing your boss's request. On your way home late that night, you find yourself holding the steering wheel in a death grip and having an imaginary conversation with Colleen. You fantasize telling her, "I give you all this flexibility, and what do you do when I really need you? I know it's tough raising a child by yourself, but it seems like you're using him as an excuse to get out of this assignment. This is just nuts! You're taking advantage of me, and I don't appreciate it." You have variations on this conversation throughout the evening.

At this point, stop reading for a minute to consider what you would do the following day. Try to determine what you would *really* do, not what you think you *should* do.

If you're a pleaser, you would probably do nothing. Having vented your anger through your imaginary conversations, you're calmer now and wondering if you have been caring enough. If you're a friend, you might still be angry with Colleen but make it a point to avoid her, fearful that she'll see how angry you are. Somehow you're convinced that if she witnesses your anger, it will harm your relationship. So you do nothing directly. But you may find yourself dreaming about small ways to punish or get even with Colleen in the future. If you're an encroacher, you are more likely to decide to talk to Colleen tomorrow. You will rehearse your strong message, but when you deliver the message, the words will not be as tough as you rehearsed them in your mind the night before.

When I asked a group of Relating managers how they would handle the situation with Colleen, the two most common responses after "do nothing" were these:

"I would ask her to try to be available to help me more when I had these emergencies."

"I would ask her if she understands the importance of teamwork and then try to show her that we need to be a team here with everyone contributing his or her fair share."

Can you feel how weak these phrases are on the Requiring scale? Note that these managers are *asking* Colleen to do what they want. Asking is not what is needed here. Your less natural skill of Requiring must be used if you want to resolve this situation effectively. Here is what a 2R manager would say to Colleen, and it's likely that it's what you wish you could say to her:

"Colleen, when you have needed flexibility, I have given it to you. When I have needed flexibility, you haven't given it to me. That has to change. I need you to be available to help me."

There is nothing unkind in this statement. A Requiring manager might say something like "Colleen, when I ask for help like I did yesterday, I need you to give it to me." I find nothing wrong with this direct a statement, but I acknowledge that it would be hard for a Relater to say. Be as direct as you can, and don't worry about showing some anger on occasion, since you probably have a good reason when you are upset with one of your people. If you're worried about being viewed as mean or nasty, recognize that this is unlikely, given your Relating style. Raising your voice once in a while isn't going to turn you into a jerk in the eyes of your people. However, it may produce some reactive efforts to make you feel guilty. Be prepared for them, and hold your ground.

To avoid being locked in to a Relating mode when dealing with direct reports, try the following approaches:

• When direct reports aren't responding to asking, relating, or hinting, you must try a more direct approach. Remind yourself that some people will say no (or say yes and do nothing) when you ask them for help, especially if they've learned there are few consequences. Just because you ask nicely doesn't mean you'll get the answer you want. Keep in mind that you have the alternative to tell people what to do. It isn't a comfortable one, yet, but it is an option.

• Substitute *I* for *we*. Relating managers shy away from saying, "I need you to do this." They prefer, "We need you," feeling that this is a less demanding way of giving someone an assignment. The amorphous *we* takes the accountability out of a request; your direct report is not accountable to you but to some undefined group of people. Often saying "I need" can work wonders. "I really need your help" or "I need you to . . ." are very effective words. They communicate that you, personally, are invested in an assignment and that you will hold this person accountable if something goes wrong. Make a conscious effort to substitute *I* for *we*.

• Recognize that your internal angry conversations affect only you. Be alert for conversations with yourself in which you are irritated with one of your people but fail to say anything to the person in real life. Certainly, there are instances when it makes sense to keep your anger inside, but if you're doing it all or most of the time, you're locked in to your Relating style. Monitor yourself for these internal conversations; then consider them rehearsals for the real thing.

The most effective and quickest route for you to learn to require of others is to learn to use assertive skills first. Chapter Eight is devoted entirely to helping you develop asserting and Requiring skills.

A SPARE KEY FOR UNLOCKING OVERRELIANCE ON YOUR NATURAL R

Although we've talked about a number of reasons people get stuck in their dominant managerial style (they believe it's been responsible for their success, using the other R instinctively feels wrong, and so on), there's another obstacle you should be aware of. Managers place the highest value on traits they are good at and have difficulty seeing value in traits they are not good at.

If you are like most people, you want to feel good about yourself psychologically. One common way of doing this is by overvaluing your strengths and undervaluing your weaknesses. If you're a Requirer, you value your task orientation and your urgency to achieve and devalue "touchy, feely" kinds of traits you are not so good at. If you're a Relater, you value your caring and listening skills and devalue bossy and overbearing traits. This value structure prevents you from appreciating people who possess the traits you lack. It becomes an obstacle in your quest to become a 2R manager because you don't want to be like people you devalue.

I saw this at Hewitt Associates every year when we went through the process of selecting which employees should become owners. We would ask every owner for evaluations of all eligible employees they worked with, and these evaluations often told us more about the evaluator than about the person being evaluated. The actuaries were positive about people who were detailed, accurate, timely in response, and thorough, less appreciative of people who were showy, loose on details, and overly aggressive. The consultants who concentrated on sales and promotion work were positive about people who could make a great impression and were socially skilled; they were less appreciative of people who were number crunchers and computer systems types. Both groups limited their own opportunities by chronically devaluing traits they did not have. Similarly, Relaters view more aggressive managers as arrogant show-offs who create conflict. Requirers perceive people-pleasing managers as time-wasting, political, and unproductive. In each case, resistance hardens to the opposite type.

At Hewitt, we saw that the best evaluators (not to mention the best managers) were the ones who valued people who had skills different from their own natural strengths. They understood that the firm needed many kinds of skills and truly appreciated people who brought strength in skills where they themselves were weak. They became more versatile themselves by being interested in and receptive to the traits they lacked. The best Relating managers valued the ability to require and wanted to become better at it. The best Requiring managers valued the ability to listen and learn from direct reports and strove to emulate it. These versatile managers were the ones we wanted to promote.

To help loosen the hold of your natural R, try the following:

• Create a list of managers you work with whose style bothers you. List the specific traits that you find irritating. Perhaps recalling your critical inner voice when you read about over-Requirers in Chapters Three or over-Relaters in Chapter Four will trigger some of the irritations you experience.

• Think about how these identified managers add value to the organization. Reflect on specific situations where these managers used their skills to solve problems (or take advantage of opportunities) that would have been difficult for you.

This exercise may allow you to be receptive to strengthening your less natural skills in order to become a more versatile manager. You don't have the negative traits you dislike in these managers. Imagine how effective you could be if you had more of their positives. Versatility is a crucial concept, and the Chapters in Part Three are designed to help you take specific steps to increase it.

Increasing Versatility

CHAPTER SEVEN

Versatility-Fostering Beliefs

T he advice in Chapter Six about getting unstuck from your primary R (as well as earlier advice about using both your Rs) revolves around the concept of versatility. I've waited to focus on this concept because you needed to become familiar with your particular type (as well as the broader 2R model) before you could put versatility into practice. Many managers feel they are versatile when in reality they are often only versatile within a narrow managerial range. For example, the demander sometimes uses fear as a motivating tactic but feels he can rely on praise as an incentive. If this manager had a better understanding of Requiring and Relating, he would recognize that his "versatility" is limited to one R. (His praise is for doing things as he wants them done and only fortifies the fear on the next assignment.)

From a 2R perspective, versatility is the ability to relate and require as circumstances dictate. Versatile managers can both obtain excellent work and help people grow. They use both their Rs, allowing them to see more alternative approaches than managers who view situations only from the perspective of their dominant R. The advantage of versatility is similar to using both hands instead of one or using the left and right sides of your brain rather than just one side. People who play the piano with both hands produce more satisfying music than people who play using only one hand. Individuals who can bring both logic and creativity to problem solving are more effective than those who can't.

Versatility isn't a denial of your natural managerial style but an acknowledgment that you have more options as a manager than you may recognize at first. It gives you the ability to behave in different ways with different employees to accomplish goals together. With some employees, taking more time and listening is what they need to grow and become more valuable to you. With others, demanding what you want will yield the best results. Knowing when to use each style and being able to use each effectively is what versatility is all about.

As simple as this concept might seem, it can be confusing in practice. Specifically, there are two misconceptions about versatility. First is that versatility is synonymous with *balancing:* trying to use your less natural style as much as your more natural style. Second is that developing versatility is *compromising:* doing something you don't want to do at the expense of doing something you feel you should do in order to be more Relating and Requiring. Versatility is neither of those things. It is about increasing your options as a manager, giving you the choice to use the approach most likely to be effective with each employee and each situation.

Increasing your versatility begins with commitment. In other words, you need to make a conscious commitment to be more versatile as a manager. To that end, I'm going to explore the belief systems of versatile managers here so that you know to what you're making a commitment. By the end of the chapter, you'll understand what versatile managers think and feel about their roles and how their belief system translates into behaviors. For example, 2R managers believe that their direct reports often know things they don't about how to best get a job done. This belief facilitates the behavior of asking and involving them in determining how to do a job.

FROM BELIEFS TO BEHAVIORS

If you believe that one of your direct reports is smart and can help you, you form an attitude about her, and your selection of words and tone with her reflect that attitude. Displaying the attitude through your words and tone helps you achieve a better working relationship with this person. The belief creates an attitude, which translates into behaviors that help you work more effectively together.

For our purposes, beliefs are assumptions you make about yourself, your employees, and your relationships at work. Even if you haven't fully articulated what you believe (to yourself or others), you harbor certain attitudes that shape your selection of words, tone of voice, decisions, and actions. An over-Requiring manager, for instance, may feel superior to her direct reports, and this underlying belief fosters an attitude that results in snide remarks, superior-sounding criticisms, and bossy orders delivered with a tone of exasperation. That tone and the words used create a poor relationship that makes it difficult for her people to find their own way to solve problems. This manager needs to adopt the belief (that 2R managers have) that she is not better than her employees—more experienced, to be sure, but not better. If she could adopt this belief, it would encourage her to behave in ways that would help her succeed. This is a versatility-fostering belief, one that would encourage her to develop her less natural behavior skills. Take another example. A versatility-fostering belief for an over-Relater would be, "I cannot please my employees all the time. I cannot leave every interaction with them feeling good about our relationship. I can trust that as time goes on, they will see that I care about them." This belief would encourage the manager to more easily hold his people accountable for their work. Perhaps the easiest way to think about a versatility-fostering belief is as a belief that would encourage a manager to use his less natural skill more naturally.

Because beliefs are not always identified or conscious, they can be significant obstacles for managers who want to become more versatile. As much as you may consciously want to access your less natural style, you find yourself falling back into your traditional behavior patterns after a while; your beliefs exert tremendous power over how you manage.

BELIEFS OF 2R MANAGERS

I have identified the beliefs of 2R managers and sorted them as versatility-fostering for different groups of managers. I want to urge you to work slowly through this section, as your beliefs are the starting point for developing your versatility.

For each belief, ask yourself if you believe it and if so, whether you demonstrate it in your managerial behavior. If you believe it and show it, that's great. If you believe it but don't show it, you now know what you need to do. If you do not fully believe it, write the belief down alongside your to-do list or highlight it to be reread later. Your goal should be to act on the beliefs you accept and consider those you don't yet accept.

Let's start with versatility-fostering beliefs for Requiring managers to help them relate with more ease.

Beliefs That Foster Versatility for Requirers

Adopting these beliefs will help Requirers have an attitude that will lead to actions and behaviors to relate more easily.

- My reports know things I don't about how best to get the job done.

- My employees may have new ideas about how to do a better job.

- I would make better decisions if I consulted with my employees and gave them the chance to react to my ideas or tentative conclusions.

- I don't have all the answers.

- My employees need to feel appreciated to do their best work.

- They need to feel they can talk to me to do their best work.

Beliefs That Foster Versatility for Relaters

Adopting these beliefs will help Relaters have attitudes that will lead to actions and behaviors to require with more ease.

- My reports cannot grow without the feedback about what they are not doing well or could do better.

- Poor performance puts extra burdens on my group and on me.

- My employees expect me to manage, make decisions, set priorities, and deal with unacceptable behavior; the conflicts this creates are necessary.

- Helping my employees grow more, even if they don't immediately like it, would enhance my long-term relationships with them.

- Asking for what I need and want is not demanding behavior; it is normal managing behavior.

Now let's look at some beliefs that would help people who need to do less Relating or Requiring. Again, ask yourself if you believe these statements and if so, do you show it in your managerial behavior?

Beliefs That Help Reduce Excessive Requiring

Adopting these beliefs will help you have attitudes that will lead you to lighten up in your actions and behaviors.

- Giving orders is not necessarily the most effective way to get what I want from employees.
- My employees will feel more respected if I let them finish their sentences and their thoughts.
- My employees will not share what they think if they feel they can never change my mind.
- I will get no new ideas if I resist and quickly argue with all the ones I get.
- My employees want to do a good job.
- Swearing, yelling, and accusing are not effective methods to get what I want.
- I don't need to feign omniscience; I can work with my people to figure out the answers.
- I would get more from my reports if I listened to their agendas before expressing mine.

Beliefs That Help Reduce Excessive Relating

Adopting these beliefs will help you have attitudes that will lead to actions and behaviors to express what you feel and think more easily.

- I am not responsible for my employees' success or failure. I can help, guide, advise, and suggest, but it is each employee's personal responsibility to succeed.
- I cannot please my employees all the time. I should not expect that every interaction with employees will leave us feeling good about our relationship. I can trust that over time, employees will see that I care about them.

• I do not have to ask my employees how they are doing all the time. I also don't have to spend lots of time guessing about whether they will like something I am doing. I can trust that if they feel something is wrong, they will talk to me about it.

• It is not helpful to worry so much about how my employees feel. They will feel good by doing good work and being part of a successful group. My decisions should be made solely on my judgment of what is best, not what most of my employees think.

• My employees need some feeling of control over the timing and length of our interactions.

CORE BELIEFS THAT PROMOTE VERSATILITY

The beliefs expressed so far foster versatility for specific management types. The following beliefs are more general and foster versatility in all management types. I've used these beliefs and attitudes at Hewitt Associates since 1970. Over the years, some of the language describing these beliefs has changed, but the principal points have remained the same. They represent core beliefs about human behavior and the managerial relationships that make versatility possible. As you look at each of the following beliefs, you may find it easy to nod and agree with what you're reading. What I would ask you to do is slow down and think about each belief. Ask yourself if your typical managerial behaviors really reflect it. Pay attention to how you feel when you read the belief (for example, is there a little voice in the back of your head protesting what you're reading?).

1. I enjoy teaching others what I know how to do.

Relaters and Requirers can both enjoy teaching. If a Relater enjoys teaching, it is easier to do one of his toughest tasks, discussing weaknesses to help people grow. If a Requirer enjoys teaching, it is easier to do one of her toughest tasks—establishing a caring or helping relationship. Reaching out to share more information, answering questions, taking employees with you to meetings, encouraging them to make presentations, and correcting mistakes are all easier and more natural if you enjoy teaching.

2. Direct reports want to achieve individually, and they want to be part of a winning team.

The most successful professional sports teams have managers (or coaches) that strike a wonderful balance between promoting stars and sacrificing some stardom for the team to function best. This is most easily seen in basketball, where there are only five players. The championship teams find ways to encourage their stars to help and work harmoniously with the specialty players. The 2R manager does the same thing, by not overhyping the best workers, by encouraging teamwork, by sharing information easily, by fostering cooperation, and by acknowledging and appreciating everyone's contribution.

3. I'm not a better person than the people I manage.

Managers may be more experienced and knowledgeable, but they should not feel or act superior to their direct reports. Versatility is facilitated by humility and equality. If you feel superior to others, you are probably locked in to opinions too strongly and are less open to letting employees help you. You are less likely to appreciate strengths that are different from yours. If you manage someone who has as much or more potential than you do, you will feel threatened by it and avoid using your full range of managerial skills to help the person realize this potential.

4. There are mutual responsibilities with each direct report.

In other words, your attitude is, "I work for each person who reports to me, and each of them works for me. I may influence their pay and promotions, but they can influence my group's performance as well as my boss's attitude toward me." When your philosophy is that managing is a two-way street, you will be more likely to focus on both your roles—getting great work done through others and helping each person grow and succeed.

5. I enjoy finishing team tasks and seeing the people I manage do good work.

This attitude may require a change in mind-set. You start out in your career trying to succeed through individual effort and determination.

Now that you are a manager, you need to shift your sense of personal gratification to others' success. This belief facilitates your insisting on quality, confronting poor performers, and setting priorities (versatility for the Relater) in addition to creating a team environment and encouraging and nurturing reports to be their best (versatility for the Requirer).

6. I want to develop as a manager—to deliver excellent work through others and help them reach their potential.

This belief necessitates acquiring additional competencies. The willingness to develop as a manager by obtaining new skills and knowledge enhances your versatility. You don't view your success as tied to just one thing, such as working harder. You believe development is a more holistic process. This attitude makes you more willing to consider learning how to use your less natural style.

7. I can learn from the people I manage.

The more you are open to what your people say, the more you can learn about yourself as a manager. Their feedback will tell you where you're falling down in the Relating or Requiring areas. They may tell the Relater to deal with the poor performer who is hurting the group or the Requirer when to lighten up to be more effective. While some of these messages may be expressed quickly or indirectly, if you listen, you can hear things that will help you achieve better results. Acceptance of and eagerness for feedback are the hallmarks of a versatile manager.

8. I respect each individual, for I know that every employee needs respect to do his or her best work.

This belief includes respecting diversity, whether your reports are young or old, male or female, black, white, Hispanic, or Asian, gay, differently abled, of a different religion, or different in any way. It includes appreciating the contribution of every employee, independent of what role they play. For Requirers, giving respect means not using power to intimidate people who serve you in your department or other departments. For Relaters, it means respecting your direct reports' ability to accept constructive criticism.

I hope you already possess these general management versatility-enhancing beliefs. If you don't accept some or want to argue with how they might be worded or want to hedge on when you do or don't believe them, you can make progress by acknowledging the truths you do accept. Our beliefs change as we acquire new experiences and information. Becoming aware of these beliefs and how valuable they are to your managerial success and effectiveness now may make you more willing to embrace them in the future.

What I hope you won't do is ignore the beliefs that don't match your own and attempt to "prove" that you can be a good manager in spite of your differing beliefs. For instance, let's say you reject belief 7 and really feel that you cannot learn anything about managing from the people you manage. These people will quickly pick up on the fact that you are not open to suggestions, with the result that you will have put some real distance between your employees and yourself. You are no longer on the same team.

THE UNIQUENESS OF EVERY RELATIONSHIP

Your relationship with each person you manage is unique. Of all the beliefs we've discussed, none has a greater impact on a manager's capacity for versatility. By accepting that each relationship is unique—and the logical corollary that you should *not* necessarily treat others as you want to be treated—you increase your ability to add options to your managerial approach. After all, why do you need versatility if your direct reports have the same needs and wants as you do?

To help you accept this reasoning, consider how different each relationship can be. Each of your people starts work with a set of attitudes about you (the authority figure) even before he or she has met you. Many experiences contributed to forming their attitudes about authority, but let's look at the issue of how they might have been raised by their parents. Based on how they were raised, we can make some reasonable guesses as to attitudes they bring into the workplace with respect to roles and relationships.

Sarah was raised by highly critical parents; as a result, she is likely to engage in critical self-talk; view you, her manager, as someone who will be critical; see you as an overseer and a corrector of her behavior; be guarded (rather than open) in her communication with you; and be critical of others.

Bill, by contrast, was raised by nurturing parents, so his assumptions and beliefs about your managerial role are very different from Sarah's. He assumes that a manager is there to help him succeed and to coach him. He is more open when communicating with you and assumes that you are on his side.

Finally, Carol grew up with parents who were emotionally unavailable (either physically or psychologically), providing her with yet another set of beliefs about what her manager is supposed to do. Most likely, Carol doesn't view a manager as an important component of her work life. Having made her way in the absence of consistent interactions with primary authority figures, she may assume that she can continue to do so in the workplace.

Obviously, these examples are based on psychological generalizations. Still, they communicate how each employee might approach a manager differently, based on strongly held assumptions about power relationships. Prior to your having any impact on them, Carol is going to view you differently from Sarah, no matter what managerial type you are.

Complicating matters, you come to the workplace with your own beliefs about what it means to be a manager. A manager raised by critical parents may believe that a good part of his role is to be a critic. He feels that the only way for him to ensure that his employees produce good work is for him to be on top of everything they are doing. Just as he believes that his kids need discipline to perform well, he feels that his direct reports need very clear rules and policies. Just as he gave his children time-outs when they were younger and grounded them liberally in their teenage years, he has "punished" reports who break his rules by chewing them out or putting them on probation.

A manager raised by nurturing parents might feel that her role is to support her people. Since she derives great satisfaction when she helps a direct report succeed, it's no wonder that she prioritizes the coaching role.

Finally, a third manager, raised by emotionally unavailable parents, might adopt a hands-off managerial style. Neither a coach nor a critic, he assigns jobs to people and then leaves them alone to do their work. He occupies a managerial neutral zone where his involvement with his direct reports is minimal.

Obviously, manager-employee relationships are much more complex than I've just portrayed them. Parenting styles may give you certain psychological tendencies, but all sorts of other events—your educational history, your previous work experiences, and your personal life—shape your views of authority and your relationships. However, the point of these personality sketches should be clear: each manager and each employee comes with a unique psychological profile, which results in a relationship different from every other.

A RELATIONSHIP THAT DEMANDS MORE VERSATILITY

Being able to require or relate as needed will help you adjust to the many different relationships you'll participate in over the course of your managerial career. Believing that you'll encounter a wide variety of people and enjoy a wide variety of relationships will make it clear that versatility is an indispensable managerial capability.

It will also help you avoid the manager's cardinal sin of adhering to the Golden Rule. Doing unto others as you would have them do unto you isn't a good idea if each of your relationships is unique. Nonetheless, many managers automatically treat their people as they themselves want to be treated by their bosses. For instance, they don't need a lot of encouragement or compliments from their managers, so why should their reports expect it from them? But unless you're reading this book in some future century, you don't have a group of clones working for you. Though some of your reports may share certain traits or tendencies, each has a unique personality that you need to adapt to. Rather than use yourself as a reference point for how to treat your people, use the 2R rule: treat each individual as an individual, and work together to ensure high standards of work performance as well as to help all of them succeed.

Though versatility is required to achieve this goal, you don't have to be a psychologist in order to "read" the psyche of each direct report. Managers don't need to know why people do what they do; they just have to focus on what they do on the job. You're not dealing with the whole personality of a direct report but how it manifests itself in work behaviors. Being versatile within this work context—rather than having to bend your managerial style into a thousand different psychological shapes—is an attainable objective.

The next two chapters are designed to help you achieve this objective. They're the prescriptions for increasing versatility, and I've divided them into separate prescriptions for Relaters and Requirers. No doubt you're going to pay more attention to the chapter that addresses your particular needs. That's fine, as long as you don't ignore the other chapter. You'll find that the chapter on your less natural R will help you increase your versatility in dealing with your employees and managers who don't share your dominant style. By learning how they can increase their versatility, you will pick up some ideas for assisting them.

CHAPTER EIGHT

Requiring for Relaters

R equiring is a difficult skill for Relaters to master. In the extreme, you must insist on what you want, whether your direct report likes it or not. Very few Relaters want to reach the point where this is necessary. Fortunately, there is an interim step of learning to assert that for many situations will replace the need to require.

Becoming assertive means finding your voice; it's the ability to say what you think and feel without guilt or concern about how others feel or react when you say it. This voice isn't cruel or uncaring. Instead, it's authentic. When you assert, you're talking straight. You're taking the initiative to articulate what you want to say. You can evaluate a situation and choose what is best for the group, independent of how many people agree with you. You can insist on your people redoing work because you know that the final product will be better. You can tell someone what she needs to do differently without worrying about the initial impact of your words.

The goal of this chapter is to help Relaters make definitive progress in developing the skills needed to improve work products and provide people with the information they need to succeed. Abdicators, friends, and pleasers all have some obstacles that prevent them from doing these activities directly and comfortably. Let's look at these obstacles and then suggest some ideas for how to overcome them.

OVERCOMING LINKED OBSTACLES

For thirty years, I've asked managers who have difficulty Requiring what they feel blocks them from doing it. Interestingly, the answers haven't changed much over this time. For each individual manager, there is a unique, personal combination of explanations from among the following:

"I've always been collegial, requiring of others seems so demanding and competitive."

"I am uncomfortable judging others; I just like to get along."

"I've never liked the emotional aspects of disagreements or conflicts."

"I have a great need to be liked."

"I have a need to avoid doing things that will make people dislike me."

"I want to be well thought of as a person."

"I don't want to hurt my relationships with my people."

"They are my friends—I don't talk to my friends in a Requiring way."

"I have never been a 'bossy' person—that's just not who I am."

"We had a lot of conflict in my house; I've always run from it."

"The idea of upsetting others to get my way seems impossible."

"I like people and do things that help them like me."

"I don't try to stand out or put my desires ahead of others."

"I'm used to reaching out to meet others' needs; I don't know how to get my needs met."

"I don't identify with the Requiring aspects of managing. I think of myself as a nice person who happens to be a manager."

"I've always been sensitive to anyone who might think I was selfish."

"I've never liked to argue, debate, or fight verbally and don't like people who seem to enjoy it."

"I don't feel that others will listen to me."

"I don't feel worthy to make these demands on others. What gives me the right to think I am right and they are wrong?"

"I don't like to criticize others, as I may be wrong."

It is likely that some of these statements match how you feel. They (and probably some not listed here) are experientially linked obstacles that lead Relaters to minimize requiring activities. Basically, abdicators, pleasers, and friends are, in varying degrees, *too far out of their comfort zone of experience to require.* A Relater feels he's the one creating the tension and conflict by taking on the issue to ask for what he wants. Even though he knows he has to exert some pressure, as a manager, to get things done well, his reluctance, resistance, and lack of past positive experiences make his efforts halfhearted. Given his experiences, the logic of his resistance is compelling. But as a manager, he is under pressure to achieve certain goals and results. How can he do things well if he doesn't learn to get more of what he wants from his people?

To overcome their resistance to assert or require, managers must (1) see the benefits of and commit to improving these skills, (2) find relatively comfortable ways to ease into doing so, and (3) build on their successes until they can feel that relationships are strengthened, not hurt, by the activity. What follows, then, are ideas and concepts to help convince you to make a sincere attempt to develop these skills, a briefing on the essentials of asserting, and a specific four-month plan to develop your asserting and Requiring skills.

BECOMING MORE ASSERTIVE— WANTING AND COMMITTING TO DOING IT

I have found that 60 percent of becoming an assertive manager is your wanting and committing to learning these skills, 20 percent is knowing how, and the remaining 20 percent is actually doing it. Here are four suggestions to help you leave your comfort zone in order to learn to assert and require.

Take Responsibility to Fully Accept the Job to Manage Others

When you were asked to become a manager, it is unlikely that the conversation covered why you might or might not want the job. But perhaps it should have. It is likely that you have not yet come to grips with the fact that the job is asking you to do some things you don't want to do. Depending on whether you're an abdicator, pleaser, or friend, the job may require you to do things that fight with your self-concept or your desire to avoid conflict.

The job demands that you strive to achieve results. A results focus will require you to engage in activities that lead to disagreements and confrontations. This isn't a guess; it's a certainty. If you haven't already done so, it is imperative that you have a serious conversation with yourself in which you either accept the role of a manager, with the understanding that you must develop a greater comfort with conflict, or decide that the role is not right for you. By making a conscious decision to accept the managing job, you are facing squarely that you need to learn how to get more from your people.

Learn to Become More Comfortable with Conflict

Other Relating managers have made this transition, and you can too. Intellectually, you probably accept that learning how to ask for more might be to your advantage. You also know that conflict is an inevitable part of life and of all sincere relationships. Remember that you're very likely to handle conflict with sensitivity because, as a Relater, sensitivity is one of your strengths. Embrace the idea of trying to be more relaxed about it. It is an opportunity to learn that asking more from people will not destroy good relationships but will actually create them.

Conversely, and equally important, trying to avoid conflict has its downside too. You know you are compromising on quality, on excellence, on helping your people as much as you should. The strategy to avoid conflict also produces discomfort. You are not doing your job as well as you can, and you know it. You have been willing to live with that, perhaps because it seems to be hurting only you.

Furthermore, avoiding conflicts with some people usually creates conflicts with others. If you don't take on a poor performer, for example, others in the group are overburdened. If you don't set priorities clearly, some jobs will not be done on time.

Finally, if someone interviewed all of the people you have ever managed, it is likely that most would say that you didn't really help them grow as much as you could have. You tried too hard to be their friend or please them, but they would feel better about you now if you had told them what they needed to hear to do their best work. You now have the opportunity to have a more positive impact on their work lives.

Create a Vision for Relating That You Can Really Get Behind

It is likely that your boss and the company, through informal and formal encouragement, would prefer that you were tougher with your people. You have resisted accommodating them, perhaps because that sort of attitude doesn't fit how you think of yourself. Your organization may emphasize numbers such as sales, productivity, earnings, and so on, and you think of yourself as a people person. One way you can bridge the gap between what others want from you and what you want to give is to have a vision for what you are trying to be as a manager, which is a better match with how you see yourself as a person.

That vision might be close to the ideal Relating manager described in Chapter Two. Ideal Relating managers are motivated to help others succeed. As a result, they provide guidance designed to facilitate strong performance. They are intent on fostering individual growth; they want to help each person reach full potential. This means encouraging an employee when she needs encouragement, supporting her when she needs support, and coaching her when she needs coaching. You care about people but often withhold information they need to grow. A caring manager tells his employee what she needs to do better, independent of whether she will like to hear it. A caring manager tackles bad performers to protect the rest of the group from the infection they bring. A caring manager doesn't just do and say what satisfies the immediate needs of his people. His approach is longer-term and more substantive: he wants not only to help his direct reports succeed in their current jobs but also to prepare them for future roles. Communicating directly and clearly how people can grow is the most caring, nurturing thing a manager can do.

Here is an exercise that might help you see this vision. Can you remember anything a parent or teacher did to you that you hated at the time but in retrospect knew to be right? These people had your best interests at heart and were willing to risk your displeasure to do something they knew was good for you. It is that kind of long-term caring that you want to offer your people.

After many years of managing at Hewitt Associates, Fred suddenly got it. He recognized the depth of influence he could have in a new way. Fred was a friend-style manager (though probably close to being 2R) of a geographically dispersed group of several hundred consultants. He had many wonderful management traits: he was intelligent and insightful, added value to every conversation he was in, had lots of ideas and expressed them well, and was interested in knowing and getting along with his people. He was also highly motivated to make sure the products from his group were of very high quality. Overall, he was a fine manager.

But he limited his potential contribution in one area. He didn't develop others. He could state how the product could be improved, but he wouldn't take the initiative to tell people how *they* could improve. In a conversation one day, I asked him why he didn't direct his exceptional insight toward coaching and developing his people more. He gave me some excuse about how people seldom really change, but he thought more about it and a few days later came back and said that his vision of his job was that of an experienced colleague but still one of the team. Because he liked being a friend to his people, he felt that coaching them would put himself "above them." But Fred was intrigued and wanted to experiment with the vision of being a greater mentor to his people. From that day on, he was a 2R manager. He had the skills all along; he just needed a new vision to apply them.

Perhaps you need to reframe your vision of what you are trying to do in the Relating side of your job. It may help to know that with your Relating style (which includes tone of voice, choice of words, and so on), you already exhibit that you care about people. Others already know this about you. If you focus your time and energies on telling them what they need to hear to do their best, it will not take away from how your people view you. It just might be something they remember you for forever.

Act on the Versatility-Fostering Beliefs for Relaters

If you accept the beliefs listed in the left-hand column, your desire to do the actions in the right-hand column should increase.

IF YOU BELIEVE THIS	DO THIS
"My direct reports need feedback about what they can do better in order to grow."	Share the information they need.
"Poor performers put extra burdens on me and my group."	Confront them earlier.
"My employees expect conflicts when I make decisions, set priorities, deal with subpar performance, and take other managerial actions."	Take these actions with more ease and less guilt.
"Helping my employees grow more would enhance my long-term relationship with them."	Make these efforts with more confidence.
"Asking for what I need and want is not demanding behavior; it is normal managing behavior."	Ask for what you want without hedging or feeling guilty.

Use these beliefs to commit to learning how to coach with more ease and comfort in order to serve your people and your company better. In the process, you'll also be doing a better job of meeting your own long-term needs.

BECOMING MORE ASSERTIVE— ACTUALLY DOING IT

What follows is a briefing of the essential aspects of what Relating managers should know to assert more effectively at work.

Being Assertive

Being assertive is not the same as being aggressive. Aggressiveness is stating one's views or desires so forcefully that it violates other people's rights and space. It is often harsh, insensitive, and uncaring. Assertiveness is gentler, more objective, the opposite of submissiveness. When you are being assertive, you are not trying to intimidate others or violate anyone else's space; you are trying to state what you see and feel in a clear, nonthreatening way. You are taking the initiative to say what you believe, observe, think, or feel.

Advantages of Being Assertive

Being assertive allows you to get more of your needs met. It allows you to be who you are, rather than looking to how others receive you. It allows you to express what you believe. It encourages you to communicate your positive and negative feelings, thoughts, and emotions in constructive ways. It helps you make decisions and choices without feeling guilty or counting how many people agree with you. It helps to enhance your self-esteem and self-respect. It helps you like yourself. Fears and anxieties are often reduced. It helps you defend yourself when others disagree or try to put you down. It is an effective way to get others to do what you want them to do without violating their rights to discuss matters and solve problems.

Assertions at Work

For a manager, there are two main types of assertions: "I" statements and "when you" statements.

An "I" assertion is a direct statement of what you think, feel, need, or want—for example, "I don't agree with that assessment" or "I think that is a great point." It might be given in defense of being challenged: "I hear what you are saying, but I still feel we risk losing market share with this pricing." Or it might just be an interjection of your opinions: "I don't want to go down that route. I think we'll lose in the marketplace." For getting people to do more of what you want, you will want to be able to use assertions in the form of statements that start out "I need," "I would like," "I'd appreciate it if," and "I want."

A "when you" assertion is a bit more complicated; it has a specific form and is used to show one of your people that he is doing something that's a problem.

"When you "	(A: whatever the behavior, action, or inaction is),
"I feel"	(B: whatever you feel),
"because"	(C: the consequences).

For example, "When you don't do what you have promised, I get annoyed, because then I have to cover for you." Or "When you don't do what you promise, I feel let down, and that leads me to trust you less regarding new assignments."

For business purposes, "when you" assertive sentences should be descriptions of your direct report's specific behavior and the consequences that he or she probably can't see. Those consequences can include how you react and feel, how a client or other department is served or disserved, or how other direct reports react. What it boils down to is being the mirror for your direct report; for example:

"When you don't show up at work, it puts a tremendous burden on me."

"When you aren't accurate, we could be seriously misleading a client, making us extremely vulnerable."

"When you don't communicate that you're struggling, I cannot solve the problem at the last minute."

Why do you have to verbalize these consequences? Your employee may be aware that there are some vague consequences, but he may not know exactly what they are or that you care about them. More important, if you say nothing, you are allowing your anger to build; keeping it submerged will not help you or your people. If you learn to get rid of these annoyances using assertive statements, you will remove a level of stress, and that will help you function more effectively as a manager. Over time, the words will come more automatically, and you will find yourself just making statements such as "I need you here on time."

In addition to statements with "I" and "when you," there are questions or requests that are assertive, as in "Why do you feel that's a good idea?" or "Wait—I'm not sure I understand yet. Tell me more." Interjecting questions and requests to clarify what the other person is saying is taking the initiative to get what you need to continue the conversation on an equal footing.

Some Suggestions About Delivering "When You" Assertions

Obviously, "I" assertions of how you feel or think are easier to make than assertions of what you want or need from someone else. And "I" assertions are generally easier than "when you" assertions, which confront a specific behavior. When making "when you" assertions, it is best to observe the following guidelines.

• *Employ a calm and serious delivery.* Your posture, eye contact, facial expressions, gestures, voice, and breathing should all communicate a calm, direct, serious message. Your intent is to communicate and be understood.

• *The behavior (A) should be specific and identifiable.* It is important not to make inferences about motive, attitude, or character. Just describe the behavior that elicits your feelings (B) and leads to the consequences (C). Try to avoid absolutes, such as *never* or *always.*

• *The expression of feelings (B) should be brief.* Use clear, precise terms: *irritated, annoyed, frustrated, worried, concerned, nervous, anxious, fearful, tense, confused,* and so on.

• *The business consequences (C) should be easy to state.* This is usually a quality, productivity, or relationship problem caused by or risked by the behavior. Note that if you can't articulate the impact of the behavior, you aren't ready to make the "when you" assertion.

• *Adapt the format to your personal style.* It can feel mechanical always to have to start a "when you" assertion with "When you . . ." Sometimes it just feels more natural to say "It really annoys me when you . . ." Over time, you will experiment with placing these elements in an order that seems natural to you, but all three are important. It is your worker's behavior that is the reason for this conversation. That behavior has an impact on you or others that you are trying to communicate. It also has business implications that the employee may not be aware of. All the elements must be conveyed to make the point of your communication as clear as possible.

Some Process Comments

Picture this scene. You assert, "When you come in late, Vince, it really annoys me, as I don't know what staffing I will have available that day," and Vince says, "I'm sorry. I will come in on time from now on." Dreamer.

Unfortunately, the process usually involves a few additional steps:

Assertion by you

Pushback by your employee (reflective listening on your part needed)

Assertion repeated, perhaps slightly modified

Pushback repeated or new pushback created, though delivered less energetically

Assertion repeated again

Perhaps some resolution, but at least understanding of the message

Typically, a "when you" assertion will elicit a response, usually a defensive one. Excuses such as "It wasn't my fault because . . ." are common responses. Sometimes the response is offensive, as in "Well, if you hadn't wasted so much of my time yesterday, . . ." This is the pushback part of the process, and your role is to listen and not get sidetracked into any of the excuses (unless they are valid and you would then change your assertion) or offensive attacks. Just listen, repeat or rephrase what the person is saying, and repeat your assertion. "In spite of what you have told me, I still get annoyed when you come in late. I need to be able to count on you." Typically, with each pushback by your direct report, the intensity is reduced until finally, he can really hear more of what you are saying to him. One of your objectives is *not* to leave your employee liking this dialogue. You want him to change some behavior, and he will probably need to stew on it some before making the change.

Some Sample Assertions

Here are some assertions that might be appropriate (or easily modified to be so) for situations you may face with your people. They are listed here just to give you a sense of how they sound. You may want to read them aloud, perhaps place a Y for *yes* or an N for *no* next to each one, depending on whether you can envision these words (as is, without hedging) leaving your lips. The tone of each statement is ideally quite flat, meaning that there isn't a lot of emotion (anger, frustration, petulance) delivered with it.

"I" Statements That Are Mildly Assertive

"I don't agree with that."

"I don't feel the same way."

"I don't feel as good about it as you do."

"I'm not sure that you answered my question. What I asked was . . ."

"I don't understand that yet. Could you clarify what you mean?"

"I don't think your suggestion will help us achieve our objectives."

"I like parts of that idea, but I see some problems with other parts."

"I'm not sure if you mean . . . or . . ."

"Stop. Please start from the beginning. I missed the context of your statement."

"Let me clarify what our priorities are."

"What problem are you trying to solve with that idea?"

"I" Statements That Are More Assertive

"I don't find that funny. Those kinds of jokes are not acceptable here."

"To make this the best it can be, I think you should . . ."

"I hear that you disagree, and I understand your point, but I still feel that this is the best course of action."

"Please don't interrupt me. This is important."

"I'd like to see you add (modify, revise) . . ."

"This is good as far as it goes. I think it can be better if you . . ."

"I am not satisfied with your performance lately. We need to talk."

"The quality of your work is very inconsistent lately. I'd like to talk about it."

"I don't feel your reaction yesterday to my asking for help was acceptable."

"I need to know what the two of you feel are the issues preventing you from working better together."

"I'm not sure this job fits your skills."

"I need . . ."

"I'd like . . ."

"I would like it if you could . . ."

"I need for you to . . ."

"I would appreciate it if . . ."

"I expect you to . . ."

"I feel you are taking advantage of the flexibility I have given you."

"At this point, I feel you are not doing an acceptable job."

"It is important that you tell me about problems as soon as you learn of them."

"I've noticed a tendency on your part to . . . This has some negative consequences that you may not be aware of. I'd like to discuss the matter with you."

"There is an item that is blocking you from achieving more of your potential. I'd like to discuss it with you."

Some "When You" Statements That Are Confrontive

"When you joke in response to my saying something serious, I get annoyed, as I cannot communicate what I want to say."

"When you tell me something will be done, I am counting on it. I want to be able to trust what you tell me."

"When you don't show up on time, it's aggravating. I don't know if you will be here or how I will get our work done."

"When you procrastinate, I don't get a chance to review your work, and I'm not sure we'll meet our deadlines."

"When you get angry with your coworkers as easily as you do, it is not helpful to anyone."

"When you don't communicate, I don't know where we stand on the project."

"When you knowingly give me incomplete work, what are you expecting me to do with it?"

"When you disagree in meetings, you do it with a tone that is not helpful. It sounds as though you think you're the only one who could be right."

"When you try too hard to relate, it tells your direct report that he is in control of the relationship."

"When you're trying to please your employee on each interaction, it is harder to tell her things that will help her grow."

In making statements like these, you're holding up a mirror so that your direct reports can see the consequences of their actions. Obviously, assertions are not the only means of communicating. Asking and answering questions and more casual dialogue are more common.

But Relaters need to develop the ability to assert when something they want to say needs to be heard.

FOUR MONTHS TOWARD BECOMING MORE ASSERTIVE

Outlined here is a four-month development program to improve your asserting skills. The idea is to grow through successive successes, to give you positive experiences and build on those until you feel and know that learning these skills is wonderfully enabling and effective. For each successive month, there are new ideas and concepts, new actions to try, some actions to continue, and status checks to show your progress. If you commit to this four-month development plan, you will absolutely improve your ability to insist on higher-quality work and, in the process, develop a healthier longer-term perspective of your relationships with your people.

The four-month plan assumes that you make assertions now, but the more your assertions challenge, disagree with, or confront others, the more hesitant and less confident you are to make them. Even though each of you starts with a differing level of comfort and ease with assertions, I think you will find the plan adaptable to fit your needs.

Month One

This is a month to heighten your sensitivity to the whole subject of assertiveness, to be aware of it all around you. It's also the right time to make a specific plan for working with each of your people.

We cannot stress enough that the goal of assertion is not "victory," but being able to express your needs and desires openly and honestly. Remember, the compulsion to win at all costs is the burden of the aggressive person [Phelps and Austin, 2000, p. 28].

ACTIONS

1. OBSERVE. Every morning, start your day with "Stay alert to assertiveness." Have it on your calendar if that will remind you. You know what assertive statements sound like. Watch how others make them. Evaluate which ones feel straight and authentic statements of

feeling, thinking, and opinion. Take note of those that border on aggressive, using loaded emotional words to influence or intimidate. Notice weak assertions, where the statement is so heavily hedged that you hardly know what is being asserted at all. Watch how the authentic ones are spoken without guilt. They are just stated, without being too sensitive about how the message will be received.

2. **OBSERVE YOURSELF.** Notice when you think an assertive thought, but don't say it. And when you do make one, notice whether you state what you really believe or hedge to make it sound nicer. Take note of circumstances where you may hesitate to be assertive, for example:

- Making decisions when you know disagreement is likely
- Giving negative feedback
- Correcting mistakes made by your direct reports
- Deciding pay raises or conducting performance appraisals
- Asking people to do what they may not want to do
- Saying no to a request
- Saying yes to a request that results in burdening others

3. **CREATE A FOUR-MONTH PLAN (4M PLAN).** Use a manila folder, and assemble the following three items:

- A copy of your completed Requiring survey. Look at the statements you rated 1 or 2, and mark the ones you want to improve in the next four months.
- A copy of the lists of sample assertions in this chapter. This is for your reference.
- A copy of the versatility-fostering beliefs for Relaters from Chapter Seven.

Then prepare the following two items (discussed later in this section):

- An assessment of your group's problems
- A separate page for your four-month goals for each of your direct reports

Group Assessment: Existing Problems. Evaluate your group today, using the following checklists. Write down your specific responses on a "group assessment: existing problems" sheet.

Inadequate Performance Issues

- Any poor or marginal performers?
- Any poor or unacceptable behavior?
- Anyone not helping the group function as an effective group?
- Anyone taking advantage of flexibility given to them?
- Any people in the wrong role—skills don't match job requirements?

Clarity of Direction

- Any individuals not knowing what they should be doing?
- Any priority setting needed?
- Any disputes needing resolution?
- Any projects not on target for satisfactory completion?

Opportunities

- Any opportunities for you to delegate more?
- Any teaching opportunities to pair up specific people for an assignment?

Your Four-Month Goals for Each of Your Direct Reports. Use a separate page for each of your direct reports. Think about each person and what he or she needs to know or do differently to be a more effective, more successful worker. Write down every area where they would improve their performance if they could change. Don't speculate on whether they will like to hear the message from you or whether they will want to make the changes needed. Next, mark which of these you would like to communicate during the next four months. This constitutes your 4M Plan for that individual. It shows not what you intend to do immediately but where you want to be four months from now.

These items can be issues such as double-checking some numbers before finishing an assignment or big themes of behavior that are blocking someone from satisfactory work. Perhaps you want to coach

Marie on two areas that you have noticed are weak: accuracy and thoroughness. With Paul, you need to address his tendency to run too far without checking in to see if he's on track. He's also spending a lot of job time on personal matters, and you would like to deal with that. You should have several items for each individual you manage.

Keep this folder handy at all times; you will refer to it continually during the four months.

4. TRY USING A FEW MORE "I" STATEMENTS THAN YOU MIGHT ORDINARILY USE. Now that you have created a list of your group's existing problems, it will be difficult to ignore repetitions of these problems that crop up during the month. When problems do emerge, experiment with some "I" assertions by choosing the ones that are easiest for you to do—not necessarily the biggest, most important ones. For example, you spot Marie being careless again and say, "Marie, I really need you to check your numbers before you say you are done."

OPTIONAL EXTRA

If you have a tendency not to be assertive with people who provide service in your home, use this first month to practice on plumbers, contractors, or other service providers you have contact with this month. Make sure you ask all the questions you want to ask, even calling back to make sure you understand how they will charge, when they expect to show up, and so on. If you have a dispute on quality or price, stand your ground. You will notice that asserting in this environment is easier, as you don't care as much about the other people's reactions. Notice also that it usually results in your feeling better by getting more of what you deserve to get.

CHECKPOINT

By the end of the first month, you should be hearing asserting everywhere. You spot assertions in your friends' conversations, on TV, in meetings, in restaurants, everywhere. You hear yourself coming out with "I" statements at the moment they are being thought. Or you catch yourself thinking of one but not saying it. Most likely, you have already started asserting more, as you can't avoid thinking about the existing problems list and the goals you have now set for each individual.

Month Two

This is the month to deal with several of the existing problems that you haven't dealt with before.

THE POWER OF "I"

As you become more assertive, it is easy to slip into using the word *we* to get your messages across. It's quite possible that you've been trained to use *we* as part of team-building courses you've taken. As a Relater, you'll also naturally gravitate toward *we*—for instance, "We need you to be more thorough on this research" or "We expect you to finish the report on time." Using the first-person plural softens the message (which is why Relaters tend to use it). When you are attempting to be more assertive, you need to use *I*—for instance, "I need you to do a better job of researching the new product" or "I expect you to finish the report on time." As you can tell, "I" statements are much more forceful than "we" ones. Initially, you may find it uncomfortable to use *I* as part of an asserting action. To ease this discomfort, try softening your statement slightly by saying, "What I need for you to do is . . ." or "What I'd like you to do here is . . ." As long as you maintain the use of the singular, you'll convey your message as you intended. If you're a friend or a pleaser, you can anticipate having an especially tough time articulating "I" assertions. Putting your wants and needs first feels presumptuous. But deep inside, you want to state your needs to your people because you're tired of keeping them bottled up. Remind yourself often that this is not only a perfectly legitimate managerial behavior but also one that will make you a more versatile and effective manager.

NEW ACTIONS

1. **USE "I" STATEMENTS.** Practice regularly using "I" statements when you want or need something.

2. **START TO TACKLE EXISTING PROBLEMS.** Start with the easiest ones on your list of existing problems. For each item, decide if you want to use an "I" assertion or a "when you" assertion or would prefer an informal talk with your direct report. Prepare for and deal with at least two of the items on your list.

3. START WORKING ON YOUR VERSATILITY-FOSTERING BELIEFS. Reread the versatility-fostering beliefs, select two of them, and take the actions they suggest.

4. PULL IN YOUR ANTENNAE. You are accustomed to listening carefully for reactions to what you say and do. Ratchet down the sensitivity of your antennae. Tell yourself this is a four-month experiment. Don't look to others for approval or agreement while you are developing your assertive ability.

5. MAKE AT LEAST ONE NEW "I" ASSERTION WITH EACH OF YOUR PEOPLE. Using the goals for each direct report, decide the easiest assertion you could make during this month that you probably wouldn't have made were it not for this exercise. The statements on the Requiring survey might give you an idea, or you might look at the list of assertions to get an idea. Decide that the next time a particular situation comes up, you are going to assert how you feel about it using an "I" assertion.

CONTINUING ACTIONS

1. LOOK AT THE 4M PLAN FOLDER REGULARLY. Take it with you to use when you get a five-minute break—while traveling, before meetings, whenever you have a moment. Write down ideas that come to mind about how you can handle these coaching opportunities. Reread the list of assertions and see if any idea pops into your mind that you know you could use with one of your people. Do it if you feel it isn't stretching too much.

2. CONTINUE TO BE SENSITIVE TO YOUR RESISTANCE POINTS. What situations or people make you hesitate to do what you know you should do?

CHECKPOINT

At the end of month two, you should be more comfortable with making "I" statements, even ones expressing needs and wants. And you should have tackled a few issues from your existing problems list. In addition, you might feel a little more distant from your people, as you are trying to be less sensitive to how they feel and more sensitive to whether their work is as good as you want it to be.

Month Three

This is the month you initiate some "when you" assertions, as needed, to get more of your existing problems handled.

THE PUSHBACK

Being more assertive will invariably produce some negative comments. Even if a direct report secretly appreciates the fact that you're finally leveling with him, he probably won't tell you that. Instead, he'll "push back" to test you and determine if you really mean it. From his perspective, you've been a Relating manager all the time you've managed him, so he may not trust your assertive behavior initially. It's also possible that your direct reports will respond angrily to your assertiveness, become unresponsive, or even pout.

If this sounds like how children respond to disciplinary measures, try to appreciate the parallel. Like kids, your direct reports need you to set limits, but they're not going to like it when you do. Don't play the game of reacting to their reactions. Avoid becoming emotionally hooked in to whatever reaction you get. If you anticipate tears, have some tissues available. If there is anger, let them get it out. If there is some blame-shifting ("That wasn't my fault; John told us to do it that way"), listen tolerantly and then bring the conversation back to the action you are asserting needs to get done or needs to stop. Each of these reactions can serve as a catalyst for change.

At some point, a direct report will probably tell you something along the lines of "I hear what you're saying, and I'll do better the next time." Your relating inclination at this point will be to make a joke or placate your direct report in some way because she's admitting a painful truth. Don't give in to your impulse to defuse the tension; you'll only dilute the impact of your Requiring action. By joking or placating, you're sending the message that you weren't all that serious about what you were saying. A simple "That would be great" will suffice.

NEW ACTIONS

1. **TAKE THE REQUIRING SURVEY AGAIN.** Can you see progress? Are you moving closer to "about right"?

2. **USE SOME "WHEN YOU" ASSERTIONS.** Using your 4M Plan folders, decide if there are any "when you" assertions that are needed to help one of your people get the information he or she needs to be a better worker. Plan it and do it.

CONTINUING ACTIONS

1. **CONTINUE TO REREAD YOUR 4M PLAN FOLDER.** Every time you look at the 4M Plan folder and think about one of your direct reports, some idea may come to mind, something you might do or say to help this person. Continue making progress on your four-month plan. Keep looking for ways to let the versatility-fostering beliefs help you. Look at the list of assertions and the retest results to direct your efforts to accomplish some of the remainder of your goals.

2. **REMAIN ATTENTIVE TO YOUR PROGRESS.** Continue to observe what is easy and what is hard for you to do.

CHECKPOINT

At the end of month three, "I" statements should feel a lot easier and more natural, while you are still feeling your way through the "when you" process. However, most of your energy is now focused on cleaning up your existing issues and accomplishing your four-month objectives.

Month Four

This is the month when you accomplish your objectives.

PREACHING WHAT YOU PRACTICE

When you mentally rehearse a dialogue with someone, get it to the real person—the right person. Whenever you feel resistance to giving feedback—a sense of discomfort about the conflict that might result—that should be your signal to move forward. Fight through your resistance with the versatility-fostering beliefs.

CONTINUING ACTIONS

1. **USE ALL THE TOOLS TO DEAL WITH THE REMAINING ITEMS ON YOUR EXISTING PROBLEMS LIST.** These items were hampering the effectiveness of your group. You have now started the process of cleaning them up.

2. **TRACK PROGRESS WITH YOUR PEOPLE.** Use your 4M Plan folder to see that your asserting objectives with each person have been reached, and congratulate yourself for making progress on an important set of goals.

CHECKPOINT

What have you learned? Are your people functioning better? Are you feeling more in control of the quality of work? Have you cleaned up the existing problems? Do you like what you have become? Have you seen some relationships grow and get closer?

I hope that with at least a few of your people, you have experienced the positiveness of what helping them more fully can do for your relationship so that you have a sense of achieving the relationship you desire over a longer time frame. I also hope that your progress stimulates you to want to learn more—to consider taking assertiveness training courses or reading some books entirely devoted to asserting. You're on your way to becoming the best 2R manager you can be.

REQUIRING WHEN YOU HAVE TO

Being assertive can help you achieve what you want as a manager most of the time. Typically, Relaters will start out with an "asking" approach to get what you want. If this doesn't work, you can assert to try to get what you need. Although this will work most of the time and make you more versatile, it won't work in every situation. 2R managers have a third option: they know how to require, even if they don't do it often.

To understand the difference—why Requiring can be far more effective in some situations than asserting—let's use a nonbusiness example. If someone were hitting your child, you would not stop with asserting behavior, merely telling the child-beater how his harmful action makes you feel. Instead, you would shout, "Stop it!"

Now let's assume that one of your people is taking advantage of you in some way. You don't want to require, so you start out with a question, for instance, "Gloria, what do you think happens when you do not deliver what you promised me?" If that doesn't work, you might shift to an assertion, such as "Gloria, when you don't deliver what you promise, I feel that you are not reliable and I can no longer count on you for help."

What if none of this works? When is it OK in your mind to require? When you tell yourself, "This has to stop now!" You're only going to demand if you care less about the short-term effect on your relationship than you care about ending a particular behavior. The importance of getting what you want must become more important than avoiding conflict. When this is the priority, most Relaters can require. Then you can say, "Gloria, when you tell me you will do something, I expect you to do it."

To enhance your ability to require, practice being less tolerant of negative behaviors. Make a conscious effort to put a stop to these behaviors sooner rather than later. After you have seen Gloria not deliver on a promise twice, take the initiative to go into Requiring mode with an "expectation" sentence. To convince yourself to reduce your tolerance, remember that bad behavior on the job affects other workers, so your actions are *caring* ones to the others. Good performers expect and need you to deal with people who are not making a positive contribution.

If a project is poorly done and must be reworked, how difficult is it to tell someone to do it over? You could start by stating assertively that it needs lots of work, specifying the problems and hoping he'll volunteer to do it again tonight. If he doesn't, however, you must say, "I need you to redo it tonight. Let's look at it again tomorrow." After becoming less tolerant of these behaviors, you have to think about how you're going to express your thoughts. Fortunately, a Requiring statement is just a slight variation on an assertion expressing need or want:

"I need (expect) you to do it today (now)."

"I need (expect) you to stop doing that now."

The addition of urgency, by expressing the assertion with a time constraint, makes it a Requiring phrase, but it is still not aggressive. These phrases are respectful of your people. I have found in my management training courses that Relaters struggle to say "I need" or "I want" with time frames attached. But sometimes you have no choice—you need the job done by a deadline. Don't hedge or qualify your statement. Allow it to stand on its own.

Finally, don't get hung up on making this statement absolutely perfect. Your words may feel awkward at first, but that's fine. The important thing is overcoming your reluctance to require; once you've broken the ice, your words will improve with practice.

CHAPTER NINE

Relating for Requirers

If you are a Requirer, you can become a more versatile and effective manager in two ways: by learning to listen better and by encouraging others more often and with greater skill. On the surface, these may seem simple things to do, but they are not easy skills for many Requirers to develop. If you intend to increase your versatility, you need to do more than tell yourself you will now begin to use more Relating behaviors. The first step is to come to terms with why you've resisted these behaviors in the past and may well resist them in the future.

RESISTANCE TO RELATING

Four general reasons explain why many Requirers resist Relating activities. First, Relating slows you down. Most Requirers tend to want what they want when they want it. Their task orientation is dominant, so activities that slow the process down are considered obstacles. Spending time on Relating feels like it takes you off task. It's a tangent from pursuing your goals.

Second, you may not trust relationships (which are often messy) as much as tasks (which are usually pretty tidy). What people say, feel, think, and mean are nebulous. Possibly as a result of your experiences, you've learned not to depend on others too much. You may also not feel sufficiently astute about psychological complexities to know how to build strong relationships with your people. In contrast, tasks are clear-cut, dependable, and measurable—you know what results you want and whether people are producing them.

Third, you may simply find it hard to understand your people. Even if you are attentive to what they do and say, you may not feel that you understand why they act as they do or what they mean.

Finally, you don't want to emulate people who relate a lot. Whether it is your inner voice or a generalized criticism of the productivity levels of "touchy-feely," "chitchatting" managers (or however you might decree them), you don't want to become more like them.

For any or all of these reasons, focusing on tasks is easier, and Relating activities are resisted or avoided. The lower your score on the Relating survey, the more concerned you are about this issue and the more you resist spending time relating. Resistance can also arise from misconceptions about listening behaviors. For instance, you may have convinced yourself that you are a good listener. Perhaps you were told that you listened well in school and counted this quality as a strength. While you may have been skilled at listening for informational content or when receiving directions, you probably lack interpersonal listening skills, a broader set of competencies than just hearing and remembering.

WHY YOU SHOULD LISTEN TO YOUR EMPLOYEES

Interpersonal listening involves paying attention to verbal and non-verbal communication, such as body language and tone of voice, as well as the difference between what people say and what they mean. It's likely that you ignore or fail to perceive these forms of communication because you are preoccupied with what you want to say in the dialogue. If you can learn to listen for understanding and resist your natural urge to judge and solve problems too quickly, you can increase your ability to relate to the people you manage.

Most Requiring managers are not adept at asking good questions for clarification. Their desire to get to solutions is too dominant. You will need to risk spending time asking and listening in order to get the longer-term results essential to your managerial success.

Complicating your task is that listening is a lost art. We don't teach it in schools, and we don't understand how important it is. Simultaneous talking is epidemic; you've probably been in meetings where conversations sound like an orchestra tuning up. Even if the talk is sequential and orderly, the second speaker is rarely responding appropriately to the first. Despite the fact that effective listening is vital for good relationships, most people lack this skill. Relating managers have the advantage of being interested in listening to others. Requiring managers are more often interested in speaking and being heard.

Perhaps the most effective way for you to hear how important listening is would be if you could hear what your most talented and productive employee would love to tell you if he were granted immunity for speaking his mind. In a fine book titled *The Lost Art of Listening* (1995), Michael Nichols describes the impact not listening has on all of us. Paraphrasing these impacts based on the complaints I've heard about Requiring managers, here's what your employee would love to say to you:

"When you listen to me, you are saying I am important. When you don't, you make it clear I am not."

"When you interrupt or finish my sentences, I want to walk right out and never come back. Give me the time to finish my thoughts—you might learn something."

"Just slow down and listen to me. It's the most important thing you can do in forging a good relationship with me. I will want to work harder for you. I will listen better to you, learn more from you, and accomplish more for you."

"When I am with someone who doesn't listen, I become angry and close down. When I am with someone who's interested and responsive—a good listener—I am energized and come alive."

"Listening to me lays the foundation for clear understanding and high-quality communication. High-quality communication increases my morale and trust. High morale and trust improve my commitment and productivity. Listening is good business."

"If you listen better, I and the others in the group will like working for you more. Enjoying our jobs more will result in better work being done."

"You should assume that your boss will hear all these messages. I am trying to give you a 'heads up' so you can change before he learns about your need to improve your listening ability."

BARRIERS TO LISTENING

Good communication between two competent people is very difficult. I speak in my own code (meanings of words), which is different from yours in some or many respects. Before the message reaches you, it passes through your decoder (or filters), influenced by your memories, perceptions, biases, attitudes, expectations, emotional triggers, past experiences, values, feelings, language, and vocabulary. Rarely is the message I send the message you receive. This is true in the best of circumstances, but for Requirers, there are added complications.

If we could go further and ask your best employee her perceptions of *why* you don't listen, some or all of the following might emerge:

"What I see as a barrier to your listening is your eagerness to tell me what I know and your seeming disinterest in hearing what I have to say."

"If you were interested in what I have to say, you wouldn't be jumping in so soon with an assumption or a judgment or a solution to a problem that I have not fully described yet."

"Sometimes you pretend to be listening by not interrupting, but your fidgeting and distractibility give you away."

"I am able to say exactly what I mean only occasionally. Most of the time, it is an approximation. Maybe I'm nervous, or maybe it isn't that easy to express difficult things. In any case, it takes some back-and-forth to clarify exactly what I mean. I need your interest and your questions for us to communicate well."

"I read that the biggest barrier to effective communication is the tendency to judge too quickly. I think you fall into that trap often. If you could dispel your judgment until you hear more, you could then put your fine problem-solving skills to better use."

Ideally, your employee has convinced you that you need to improve your listening skills. The process of doing so must begin with becoming more interested in what your people have to say. If you just go through the motions to appear more interested, your ruse won't work. You may fool them into thinking you're listening once or twice, but very quickly they will spot the telltale signs of disinterest. When you clearly don't remember what they told you during your last conversation or when your voice says "I'm listening" but your body language indicates otherwise, you'll reveal your true agenda—to get back to your work.

But how do you become more interested in what they have to say if you're not interested to begin with? This is not a trick question but a challenge for all Requirers. Fortunately, there is an answer. For Requirers to become effective listeners, you need to "downshift to understand" and use two sets of skills to do it.

DOWNSHIFTING TO UNDERSTAND

When you want to slow down a car with a standard transmission, you shift to a lower gear. If you want to be a better manager, you also need to slow down, to a gear we will call "U" (for *understanding*). When you are in U, your sole job is to understand what your direct report means to say to you. Instead of thinking of it as "listening better," which triggers your resistance, think of it as a problem-solving task to decode what he means to say to you. Your purpose is to refrain from replying and from solving what you perceive the problem to be (as most Requirers with automatic transmissions do). It is simply to understand.

By being in U with your employees, you are more than halfway toward effective listening, because in order to understand, you will more naturally do things that lead to effective listening. You are a problem solver and a task fulfiller. What would you do if the *only* task in front of you were to understand? You might easily respond with the following action plan:

- Become attentive to what is being said
- Ask for clarity when something is unclear
- Hold back what you have to say
- Learn to recognize and repress the urge to interrupt or argue
- Give up the interest in yourself and get into the experience of the speaker
- Resist the reflex to judge quickly what the speaker should do
- Slow down your pace and your desire to dispatch the issue

By responding in these ways, you will have adopted the principles of effective listening and improved your Relating ability. After you become more skilled at understanding, then you can react, suggest solutions, ask if your employee has a solution to offer, or decide an issue yourself. Whatever action you take once you've made an honest effort to understand will be more on target than if you had not made this effort.

To help you understand, focus on developing two sets of skills: attention and elaboration. The former will help you concentrate on the speaker and eliminate distractions (both internal and external). The latter involves asking for more information or clarification—a clear sign that you're listening actively.

ATTENTION SKILLS

When people talk to you, they want you to focus on what they are saying; they want your attention. This doesn't just mean that you say "uh-huh" every so often or repeat something they've just told you. People want you to listen with your whole body. Giving your attention means nonverbally communicating that you are interested in hearing what they have to say. Your posture, eye contact, and gestures are all "read," whether or not you're aware of it. How you position yourself during a conversation as well as your willingness to eliminate distractions influence the other person's perception of your attentiveness.

Being attentive is a talent you need to develop. Think about people who have this talent—when they are with you, they are totally with you. Here's what these people most likely do:

- They face you squarely and look at you.
- They make no extraneous movements with face or body.
- They wait for you to speak.
- They do not interrupt you or complete your sentences.
- They appear alert and interested in what you have to say.
- They seem to hear every word.
- They don't allow others to interrupt.
- They don't appear to have another concern in the world.

That's how you want your direct reports to describe you when you are listening to them. Keep these traits in mind, and practice them. Within a very short time, you will be able to see and feel the positive impact these actions have on your relationships.

To test your own capacity to be attentive, here's how managers who are oblivious to their people's ideas and concerns act. See if you do any of these things:

- Never look at the other person when he or she is speaking
- Tap your pencil, doodle, or play with something to show impatience
- Become distracted by noises or thoughts of what else you should be doing
- Do most of the talking even if the other person initiated the meeting
- React quickly before the person finishes what he or she came to say
- Interrupt or finish the other person's sentences
- Stand up and walk around
- Take calls while meeting with or conversing on the phone with the other person
- Ask the person to repeat something because you just missed it
- Fold your arms in front of you
- Yawn
- Have a radio on and occasionally hold up your wait-a-minute-finger and say, "I love that song" or "I need to hear the traffic (or weather) report"

Do you have any of these habits? That's really all they are, and you can break their hold by creating new attentive ones.

ELABORATION SKILLS

After you've worked on becoming more attentive, you're ready to develop elaboration skills that demonstrate that you want to completely understand what the other person means. People shut down if they feel you're not interested in hearing anything more than a brief answer to a question. As a result, they're reluctant to put the answer in context, to take a risk and suggest a new, related idea, or to provide a provocative observation. All of these extended responses can be tremendously valuable to managers. They contain the creative and perceptive data that can enhance the group's productivity in unexpected ways. They also contain contextual information that can give a manager a much more accurate way to evaluate a situation. Finally, they provide managers with a fuller understanding of a direct report—his strengths and weaknesses.

To develop this elaborating skill, practice using the following two techniques:

Sharing Nods, Smiles, and a Few Encouraging Words

These may seem like small things to you, but they're magnified by your managerial position; your direct reports are highly sensitive to what you say and do. A few encouraging words and facial acknowledgments communicate that you are paying attention. "Yep, I hear you. . . . I agree. . . . yes . . . right. . . . Then what happened? . . . For example? . . . mm-hmm . . . uh-huh" are all messages that tell your direct report you are with him and wish for him to continue talking.

Several Relaters in my management training courses described bosses or colleagues who failed to give any of these "continue" messages. They were presenting a report or explaining a problem and were met with stony silence—no reaction at all. Or while they were talking, the body language of their boss communicated impatience, as if to say, "Get on with it—I've got other things to do." In essence, the boss is saying, "Your concerns aren't worth my time." Requirers need to keep this image in mind to encourage them to provide relational responses.

Asking Brief, Clarifying Questions to Understand Better

Most people don't say exactly what they mean. It's too easy to make false assumptions based on what you *think* the other person means to say. It's also possible that your direct report is nervous or uncertain and his words don't convey what he really wants to communicate. Look for natural pauses in his responses where it feels acceptable to ask for clarification. Sometimes people launch into the middle of a story and you don't understand the context. Sometimes pronouns aren't clear and you can't follow who said what to whom. Sometimes you aren't sure why you are being told something—whether the other person wants you to take action or just be informed. All these items and many more can be clarified by your asking good questions that show you are interested in *understanding* what the other person is trying to communicate. Your direct report will appreciate the opportunity to say what he means. Remember, your role is to stay in U gear and understand.

If you've read any of the literature on effective listening, you've probably come across the term *mirroring skills*. These are skills that play back or paraphrase what people just said so that they know you are hearing them well. For instance, let's say you're an MIS manager, and your direct report is complaining about someone in marketing not checking with him before promising the client a software update. After hearing this complaint, you might say, "The marketing people promised the client new software without checking with you?"

As useful as mirroring skills are at showing you are listening, most Requirers feel "phony" when they try to use them. These mirroring words often stick in their throat. Even if they are able to say the words, they come out with a hollow, insincere ring. It's not that Requiring managers can't master mirroring skills, only that it's much easier to master if someone is teaching you how to mirror. If you have an opportunity to take a course in these skills, take it. For now, I'd recommend that you not try to master mirroring skills on your own. By focusing on understanding, you will naturally improve your attentive and elaboration skills, which will in turn enhance your mirroring ability, and you won't end up sounding like you don't mean what you're saying.

A STORY WORTH LISTENING TO

When I taught a class at Northwestern University's Kellogg Graduate School of Business, one of my assignments asked students to interview people who felt differently than they did on an important public issue. Declarative sentences about how the student felt were not allowed; only questions to understand what the other person was saying were acceptable. Based on these interviews, each student had to write a paper on what was learned from the process of asking questions, listening, not judging, and asking more questions. (You can appreciate the parallel when you are in U gear.)

One student chose the issue of physician-assisted suicide (PAS) for the terminally ill, which he believed should be a legal right. He interviewed people who were opposed to PAS for the terminally ill and asked questions, listened, resisted judging, and asked some more. His paper summarizing what he learned was impressive.

He learned that some of the people opposed PAS on purely religious grounds as an act that overruled God's will. Others didn't have strong arguments and started to modify their opinions just from the questions he asked. Within a few minutes, one interviewee was defining some circumstances where it might be OK in her mind. Another interviewee had a terminally ill grandmother who was perfectly willing to request a physician's help in committing suicide in order to save the family thousands of dollars a week in hospital costs; she couldn't stand being a burden to the family. The student understood that many grandparents might feel this way, even if they weren't deathly ill.

This realization helped the student begin to modify his thinking on the subject. In addition, some people he interviewed were able to clarify under what circumstances they felt PAS would be acceptable. In all cases, the student understood the person and the person's real beliefs better after the questioning and listening. Before this exercise, this student—who was very bright and aggressive with strong Requiring tendencies—would have interrupted and tried to convince others why they should share his belief.

The lessons of this story for Requiring managers are as follows:

1. If you are telling others how you feel, you can't learn anything. You already know how you feel.

2. You aren't likely to persuade others to your viewpoint no matter what you say. As the student discovered, asking questions allows people to revisit their beliefs as they mull over their answers. Some of them realize that their views aren't strong or need qualifying. When they realize this on their own—as opposed to someone telling them—the effect is much more powerful. Then they may be open to changing their minds.

3. Only by listening and asking can you gain some insight into the other person. At the very least, you will understand where to direct your arguments to have a chance of influencing the other person's opinion.

4. You might learn something that deepens and modifies how you previously thought about the issue.

If you want to establish rapport with your people, you'll engage in this process of questioning, listening, withholding judgment, and asking more questions. Not only will this active listening approach communicate that you really hear what the other person is saying, but it will help you analyze your own viewpoint as well.

LEARNING TO ENCOURAGE OTHERS

Now let's turn to the second major skill Requirers must master in order to become more versatile: encouragement. Encouraging direct reports is perhaps the most powerful motivational tool to get people to produce their best work. Unfortunately, encouragement often feels unnatural to Requirers. Without a significant mind shift, you will probably find it difficult to use this skill effectively. The problem is that you have always enjoyed looking good to others. Your psychological "driver" is to have others think highly of you and your achievements, intelligence, competency, and so on. Being the center of attention comes naturally. Encouraging others, however, is almost the opposite; it entails selflessly helping others be their best. It is not about looking good yourself but about recognizing and nurturing it in others.

"Encouraging" as I use it here has several facets: the literal meaning, giving courage; nurturing—helping someone grow; and reinforcing—expressing admiration and appreciation.

When you set out to encourage an employee, it is helpful if you can envision what this employee could become in the future. If you see basic fundamental intelligence and motivation, it is easier to imagine a fine future for this employee. Resolve to help make it happen, starting out by accepting the skills and abilities he currently possesses and your commitment to help him increase them. First, provide day-to-day teaching of what to do. Second, identify longer-term traits and behaviors that are blocking him from greater success. Third, try to find ways to appreciate his positive contributions even though they are not yet what you fully expect or want. Finally, in spite of setbacks and issues, believe in him and show it.

All this may make intellectual sense, but your natural reaction as a Requirer is likely to show itself as some form of impatience. You may still have a gap to bridge between knowing the right thing to do and doing it. That may be because you don't yet understand what happens if you fail to encourage, specifically why you resist doing it, and how you can overcome your reluctance.

RECOGNIZING THE CONSEQUENCES OF NOT ENCOURAGING OTHERS

As stated earlier, many Requiring managers simply aren't aware of how withholding encouragement affects their people. Here are some of the most common negative consequences to reflect on (you may note that some of these match the feelings your employees have when they are not listened to):

- If you do not appreciate your direct reports' talents and contributions, they will not feel as good about themselves at work. (You are not responsible for your people's self-esteem, but you can and do have an effect on it.)
- If they feel you are interested only in getting tasks done your way, they will not be comfortable making suggestions.
- If they feel they are unlikely to do right in your eyes, they will be hesitant and less confident.
- If they feel that you take them for granted, they do not feel important or unique.
- If they don't feel appreciated because of your lack of encouragement, they are likely to conclude that they won't be treated fairly.

All of these items can lead employees to assume (with some logic) that you don't care if they stay or leave. They don't appear to bring anything to work that you appreciate. Why shouldn't they prefer to work for a manager who does?

IDENTIFYING WHY YOU RESIST ENCOURAGING OTHERS

There are many reasons why managers resist encouraging others; some from the following list probably apply to you.

- *High standards.* Having high standards is a great attribute. But it can also cause you to withhold approval. People with high standards

- A handwritten "nice job" note in response to something they did or wrote

- A word of praise for at least part of something they did, as in "great summary to your presentation, Jean" (even if you believe the presentation could have been better)

- A smile of confirmation after a job well done

- Observing people doing things you like and telling them so

- An e-mail note complimenting them on something they did (Did you know that almost all e-mail compliments are saved?)

- Listening to an idea from your employee of how something can be improved with interest, questions, and attentiveness

- Asking a direct report to think about and help you with an idea of yours, demonstrating you value his thinking

- A pay raise or bonus that meets or exceeds expectations

- Including someone in a group she was excluded from before

- Providing feedback about how people can do better in a positive, future-oriented way

- Reporting positively on a meeting at which someone was responsible for some aspect (such as a presentation)

- Thanking direct reports, being specific about what you appreciate

- Asking how a meeting or presentation went and listening to the answer with no other agenda

Don't treat these items as just another list of minor activities to consider. Each one is personal and can have an enormous impact on how appreciated your people feel.

Encouraging, like listening, takes practice. The more you incorporate it into your everyday behavior, the better at it you'll become. Compliments have more impact when they're specific rather than general. It's much more effective to say, "I thought it was very smart of you to spend that hour talking to the salespeople about the new customer goals we've established," instead of, "You did a good job with the salespeople today." You'll also discover that although there are times when it's necessary to hedge a compliment, as in "You did a good job by . . . , and it could have been even better if . . . ," you should more often let your people enjoy an undiluted compliment. Sometimes your direct reports need to bask in unreserved, unqualified praise; it motivates them to work hard in the hope of enjoying such praise again.

You can become even more adept at encouraging others if you work harder at encouraging yourself. As a Requiring manager, sometimes you need to give yourself a break. When you find yourself being self-critical, lighten up and understand that you aren't perfect. When you improve on a skill or come up with a good idea, make it a new habit to compliment yourself. Although complimenting may never become second nature for you, it can be something you will feel comfortable doing more often.

As you attempt to put these and other encouraging actions into practice, you may find some habitual thinking getting in the way—for example, focusing on what went wrong rather than what went right or judging people's work in comparison to seasoned professionals when they've only been on the job for a few months or years. These are habits that can be used to develop "triggers" that shoot you into new, more versatile thinking.

Thinking about what went wrong can trigger thinking about what went right.

Obviously, you need to think about both: the former helps you understand what you need to correct for the future, and the latter puts mistakes and problems into perspective. If you're always thinking about what went wrong, you won't have the impulse to encourage because you're so focused on the negative. Encouragement occurs when you see what went right, even if other things went wrong.

Be sure the standard you are applying is appropriate to the situation.

Whenever you are appraising people or work, ask yourself, "Am I using an absolute standard or one appropriate for the employee's level of experience?" Requiring managers often establish absolute standards for performance that are unrealistic; they expect people to excel who are not sufficiently experienced. Their motivation to encourage, therefore, is minimal since performance seems to be below par. The best way to develop people is to have a vision for what they can become and persistently encourage them to take the necessary steps to get there.

In a very real way, Requiring managers need to prime the encouraging pump. Once you see the positive reaction, you'll find it just a bit easier to give another compliment next time. From personal experience, I can testify to the truth of that statement. As CEO of Hewitt Associates, I was cheap with encouraging comments. It took ten years before I understood how important my encouragement was to the people who reported to me. As I allowed myself to give more to others, I could see the enormous motivating effect it had. Though I then made a conscious effort to encourage more, I was never as good at it as I was at coaching and listening. I'm convinced I would have been a more effective CEO if I could have overcome my barriers to using this particular Relating skill.

THE REQUIRING MANAGER'S TO-DO LIST

The encouraging and listening skills I've discussed here are ones you need to think about and exercise consistently. Throughout the chapter, I've suggested different ways of incorporating these Relating behaviors into your repertoire. To get you started and create new habits, I'd suggest that you have the following reminders printed at the top of your to-do list.

- "Catch someone doing something right today," as the authors of the *One Minute Manager* (Blanchard and Johnson, 1982, p. 39) prescribed. Observe your people, and note when someone has done something—even a simple task—efficiently, creatively, quickly, or productively. Compliment the person about it.

- Stop what you're doing when your people want to talk to you; devote your entire attention to them. Refuse to answer the phone if it rings.

- Remember that your first priority is solely to understand what your direct report wants to say to you. Then you can resolve issues and create opportunities.

As you incorporate these actions into your routine, you're going to be reshaping your managerial style. This doesn't mean that you're suddenly going to become best buddies with your direct reports. It simply means that you're adding Relating alternatives to your managerial options, helping you improve your relationships with your people to become a much better manager. You're becoming more versatile, not transforming yourself into your opposite. As you'll discover, incorporating more Relating into the way you manage can take you and your people a long way.

CHAPTER TEN

When to Relate, When to Require

T o this point, I've focused on why and how you should develop your less natural skill. As critical as that effort is, the concept of versatility includes one more skill—the ability to know when to relate and when to require. This will take some practice, but this chapter will accelerate your learning through some examples and guidelines.

The most important consideration regarding when to relate or require is that the situation is the determinant. It isn't about your natural style. Your employees' actions and performance, your previous actions in working with them, and your objectives for the individual and the group are the determining factors for deciding when to relate and when to require.

SOME INITIAL GUIDELINES

• *If your people aren't performing up to minimum standards, you must require more.* For example, your direct report is not careful enough, regularly makes errors of fact, doesn't put enough thinking into his work, and so far is not performing in a satisfactory manner. You may have tried hinting and then asserting that the work is not good. Now you need to raise the volume and state clearly what you want, need, and will do if the problem is not corrected.

• *If your people need help in reaching their potential, you must both relate and require.* You know many specific things your employees need to do to grow in their jobs. You need to be able to tell them in ways they accept. This demands that you relate enough to be heard and trusted, state your objectives unambiguously, and clarify the areas they need to develop. You will need both Relating and Requiring skills.

• *Most managerial functions are done better if Relating (especially listening) is done first and Requiring second, as needed.* Decision making, performance management, objective setting, conflict resolution, problem solving, and creating a team environment are all enhanced by listening first. By asking questions and listening to the answers, you can determine if your people are resisting, rebelling, struggling with an assignment, exhibiting new behaviors, offering ideas, on the verge of leaving, or going through a personal crisis. But after you have listened, decisions must be made and priorities set for the group to move forward.

• *If what you are doing isn't working, remember your less natural R.* This was the theme of Chapter Six, "Getting Unstuck," but is worth reiterating here. The Relater feels the problem may be his fault and tries harder to relate. The Requirer feels he hasn't been clear enough and spells out what he wants even more explicitly. When you have tried but not solved a problem, Relaters should ask themselves, "Should I assert or require now?" while Requirers should ask, "Should I ask, listen, acknowledge, encourage, or compliment now?"

TWO GOLDEN OPPORTUNITIES

By using the guidelines just given, being conscious of both Relating and Requiring options, and practicing using both skills in different situations, you'll become more confident about when to use each R. Two situations offer managers versatility opportunities that are often ignored. Let's look at each situation to learn when is a good time to relate or require.

A New Person Joins Your Group

First impressions count for a lot. If you use only your natural style during the first few days or weeks of a new hire's tenure, you're going to set up expectations that are counterproductive. If you're a Relater, you could easily miss the opportunity to clarify what you expect from your new report. This will start you down the path of not confronting poor or marginal performance. If a Relater can clarify the goals and objectives for the group and expectations for the new employee, it will be much easier to confront issues later.

If you're a Requirer and use only Requiring behaviors with a new hire, you might send the message that you're a demanding and controlling type whom people can't talk to when they have concerns about their assignments, jobs, or careers. You'll miss a great opportunity to establish a positive relationship from the outset. Take some time to welcome new people personally.

2R managers make it easier to manage in a 2R way—they meet with the new person, establish rapport, set expectations, and reiterate organizational and group missions. If the first few days capture the heart and mind of a new person and clarify expectations, retention is easier, performance is better, and the manager's job will be far less time-consuming.

A Direct Report Is Having a Personal Crisis

A personal crisis is a time of immense importance to your employee. At such times, work will always take a backseat, and your handling of the situation may well determine if he comes back to work at all or works with you forever. This is a time when you need to relate. The employee needs your support, understanding, and flexibility. He may not be able to tell you what he needs, so you may have to talk to others to find out. A parent's death, a child's accident, a divorce, or a serious illness in the family can all be life-altering or devastating events. They call for Relating approaches where managers listen, empathize, and offer support.

In 1985, when *The 100 Best Companies to Work for in America* was being updated, the authors asked us why we should be included again. Our contact person, Chris Seltz, suggested that we should just ask our people for the reason. She sent out a request on our office e-mail in the morning. Within a few hours, she had over two hundred personal stories of how we had helped people manage their work and personal crises and how committed they were to Hewitt Associates. Chris was able to send the authors a copy of these stories the next day. Reading them was the single proudest moment in my career at Hewitt. We were not just giving lip service to caring about people. We were caring when they most needed it. We were included in the next edition and in every updated edition for the next ten years.

There are some other ways to create strategies regarding when a manager might want to relate or require more or less. One is to consider what happens if you are the same or the opposite type as your employee, even if he or she isn't yet a manager.

KNOWING WHEN BY KNOWING EMPLOYEE TYPE

You probably have a good feel for whether each of your people would be inclined toward being a Relating or Requiring type of personality. Might this have an impact on when you relate and when you require? Let's examine the possibilities.

Relating Manager, Relating Employee

The opportunity here is that your employee is trying to please you. Let him. You don't have to compete for who can please the other more. It should be easier for you to coach him, since he wants to respond to your advice. The problem is that it is too easy to be friends, which makes it harder for you to do the Requiring things when they are needed. The danger in this relationship is that the two of you will spend too much time enjoying each other. Maintain a professional distance to take advantage of this opportunity and still have a fine working relationship.

Requiring Manager, Requiring Employee

Your employee is already task-oriented. All you must do is guide and channel her efforts. It should be easier to relate and get her opinions, as you know she will not waste a lot of your time or hers. You can listen and encourage her more easily. If you recognize this opportunity by lightening up the Requiring and using your less natural R, the relationship should be terrific. You are both able to be direct, so discussions on problems should be relatively easy. One problem may be that it's so easy for both of you to get straight to the task that you lose input from other employees. You will need to reach out to others to avoid having the two of you form an enclave within your group.

In both of these situations, where the managers' style is matched by the employee's, the manager is not inclined to use his less natural R, because a like-minded employee reinforces one's natural style. When this happens, it may have a negative impact on others in the group.

Relating Manager, Requiring Employee

The chances of running into problems here are high as you try harder to relate and your report resists your efforts. But since he is task-oriented and will tell you what is on his mind, you don't need to relate a lot if he is doing good work. Use your natural style to complement and reinforce his work. If, however, his work or his behavior needs correcting, it is imperative that you take action promptly. If you do not establish yourself as the manager, the employee will control this relationship.

Requiring Manager, Relating Employee

The likelihood of difficulties here too is high. Your employee is likely to perceive you as even more Requiring than you are. You are also likely to view her desire to relate with you and others as a waste of everyone's time. This is a classic misfit. Nevertheless, you can help your employee achieve her best by watching your tone when you require. If your tone is compassionate, your report wants to please you and will listen to what you want. Require lightly is the message.

In both of these situations, where the managers' style is not matched by the employee's, it is important for you to use your more natural R less and your less natural R more in order to get along successfully. In all four situations, it is important to be able to use your less natural R more. Of course, that is why you have committed to becoming more versatile.

KNOWING WHEN BY KNOWING YOUR MANAGERIAL TYPE

Your natural style has a powerful hold on your behaviors, and while you may develop a good sense of when to relate and when to require, you may also revert to type under stress or when the previous guidelines no longer are as prominent in your mind. To guard against this possibility, consider the following strategies based on the nine managerial types.

The Abdicator

Because you manage minimally, your problem is not so much knowing when to require versus when to relate as doing more of both. You need to make a commitment to spend more time managing. Realistically, however, you're going to be challenged just being a more hands-on manager, and it may be asking too much to expect you to relate and require with true versatility. If you feel that this describes you, simply try to use your natural style more when you start devoting more time to managing. After you feel comfortable spending additional hours on managing, you can work on becoming more versatile.

The Friend

When you need something you're not getting from your people, consciously decide to stop Relating and start asserting. You relate about the right amount, and your talent for listening and encouraging will prompt you to use your Relating skills when you encounter problems where you should be assertive. Here are some common situations where friends mistakenly use Relating instead of Requiring skills:

- When someone is ignoring the policies and procedures you've established
- When you know someone is taking advantage of you
- When an employee is struggling to do an acceptable job
- When you're making excuses why a direct report didn't perform well
- When you have asked an employee to stop a particular behavior but he has ignored or only given lip service to your request

Check yourself from doubling your Relating efforts to get people to shape up and force yourself to use Requiring behaviors.

The Pleaser

While the strategy for the friend also applies to you, you are much more likely to use Relating behaviors to an extreme extent. As someone who tends to relate too much and require too little, you will naturally approach most situations by listening and talking empathically. You need to become more aware of situations where Relating isn't effective.

Because you're a great listener, capitalize on this ability by really hearing what people are asking of you. If you listen closely, you'll be able to hear that some direct reports don't need or want you to relate in certain situations. They will exhibit impatience or give short answers to your questions. When their conversation revolves around gaining very specific information about due dates, formats, policies, and goals, you can bet that they want explicit directions. Consequently, try to reduce your tendency to ask questions and relate. Put additional time between Relating behaviors. Use all the devices of Chapter Four to help you. Justify this reduction to yourself by noting that now you'll have more time to get your work done. Pleasers frequently fall behind because they've invested so much time in conversation with their people.

The Supervisor

Look for opportunities to relate more, as in the following situations:

- When your people make flip comments or snide remarks or jokes about not being appreciated
- When you discover a problem that everyone else already knew
- When you feel resistance from almost everyone to your directives
- When you receive very few suggestions from your employees about how to do things better
- When your best employee wants to transfer or leave the company

These are all clues that you have not been close to your people. Reach out, ask questions, and listen more attentively. Use all the tools in Chapter Nine to help you. In the past, you may have responded to these situations by showing irritation or reprimanding or just pushing harder. Try varying your approach, viewing each situation as an opportunity to sit down and have a meaningful discussion about the specific issues involved.

The 2R Manager

Because of your capacity to relate and require, you probably need only review the guidelines discussed earlier in order to use each R at the appropriate time. Certain situations might confound you, since you have to make a choice between two skills you know you possess. But since you have the capacity for both Requiring and Relating, you have more conscious decisions to make about which skill to use in each situation. Recognize that certain common managerial functions—decision making, conflict resolution, goal setting, problem solving, managing poor or marginal performers—are performed best by starting with your Relating skills and switching to Requiring when necessary.

The Encroacher

Your challenge is deciding when you shouldn't relate. Here are four signs that you may be Relating too much and should find a way to back off:

- When you want to be with people and are looking for a reason to justify it
- When you realize that the last few times you interacted with one of your people were all due to your taking the initiative to see or call him
- When you find yourself trying to control how someone feels about you through your Relating skills, such as asking how the person is doing, how the project is going, or if there's anything you can do to help (these are all good questions as long as the motivation for asking them is a sincere interest in the answers)
- When you observe "backing up" behavior by your reports (short answers to your questions, impatience to get back to their work, not returning your phone calls quickly, and so on)

The Demander

Your tendency is to demand that people solve problems by doing things your way or by working harder, even though some of these problems can't be solved this way. You also may require by using strongly worded demands that might be taken as threats when in fact you could help people get past an obstacle just by talking with them. If you charted your managerial behaviors over a period of time, you'd find you spend a disproportionate amount of time in Requiring mode. When you encounter a difficult situation, stop yourself from automatically approaching it the same way you've always done. Think about how you reacted in the past and if your Requiring style worked then. If you remember that it failed, you may be more willing to shift your approach to Relating. As a natural Requirer, you want results, and it may be that in certain situations, Relating will get you those results far better than Requiring.

Demanders are not aware that every interaction with their employee is on two levels, the content level of what you are working on together and the relationship level, when you are either building or destroying trust. Are your Requiring actions helping you build a trusting relationship, or are they hurting you? Can you consider adding more Relating activities to help you?

The Energizer

Your zeal for getting results and your high-octane personality may cause you to forget that there are situations where you should not require. Unlike the demander, your Relating skills are good, and you often use them appropriately. There are instances, however, when your natural Requiring style takes precedence because you're so hyper about achieving goals. Beware of this tendency, and consider Relating options in the following situations:

- When you are angry (your anger is likely to make you say things in particularly harsh ways that you will not be able to undo or take back)

- When a direct report is trying to get you to listen to her (you can see her struggling—sometimes desperately—to grab your attention and force you to take her complaints or ideas into consideration)

- When you're not sure of the solution (don't pretend you are sure and "act firmly" just because you are the manager; instead, use your people as sounding boards and test their reactions to your ideas, soliciting their ideas in turn)

The key shift is for you to slow down your pace in order to use your Relating skills most effectively.

The Overwhelmer

You are heavy-handed in both your Relating and your Requiring. You may know when it's appropriate to use each R, but you use them to such an extreme extent that you negate the value of using the appropriate managerial style. Consequently, when you feel the need to relate, do not smother people with your empathy. When you feel the need to require, don't steamroll your people in an attempt to get them to do your bidding. Keep the phrases "light touch" and "lower the volume" in mind when it's time to use either R. When you manage people in different situations, remember that it's not all about you; your managerial skills are only as good as your ability to use them with discretion and moderation.

REACTIONS TO YOUR CHANGES

Remember, it is human nature to resist change. Even when a situation improves, people cling to what's familiar. Therefore, don't expect applause, and do expect efforts (conscious or not) to get you to revert to your old behavior.

If you're a Requirer, your direct reports will not notice the change immediately. They are used to seeing you in a certain way and have decided what kind of manager you are. New information that contradicts their existing views will probably not register for a while. When they do notice, they won't trust that it's for real. They'll think it's an aberration, and you'll return to being who they think you are. Only after some repetition will they start to accept that you are changing.

You may or may not get a comment or compliment from them about your change, even if they like what you are doing. But you aren't changing to get compliments; you're changing to improve *your performance.* You do this by first serving your employees better, which in turn serves you. By taking the time to relate, listen, understand, nurture, encourage, and compliment, you will in turn get more help from your people.

If you're a Relater, you can expect that your direct reports will notice quickly, as you will be more assertive or more Requiring. However, they will not trust that you mean it and will try to test you, sometimes by doing things they never did before. For example, if you confront someone who has been getting away with a lot, he may come back to you with some wild new excuses to gain your sympathies or accuse you of not caring to see if you really mean to be tougher with him. He is very unlikely to compliment you on the change in how you are managing, even if he sees the benefits of what you are now doing.

Your manager is unlikely to see the changes quickly and reinforce your versatility. It may feel temporarily as if you are alone in this change. The truth is, you are. For this reason, you may want to partner with someone who you know wants you to be tougher. It might be a direct report who has asked you to handle some problem you were avoiding. Tell this partner that you are trying to make changes and want her feedback. This will help you get the positive reinforcement you need to stay the course.

For both Relaters and Requirers, once your employees come to trust the change, your relationships will improve. Your employees will see that you are using more ways to solve problems, involving them appropriately, and moving the group forward to accomplish more together.

SITUATIONAL PRACTICE

A certain amount of trial and error is involved in becoming astute about when to relate and when to require. Expect to make some mistakes. You'll find that as you practice your two styles in different situations, you'll learn what works and what doesn't. While I can tell the Requirer that you should relate when you need to mine your team for great new ideas, once you've experienced the efficacy of this new behavior, you'll be much more willing to incorporate it. The Relater will need to experience how confronting small issues earlier prevents bigger issues later on before wanting to do it regularly. At some point down the road, knowing when to relate or require will become second nature. Let's now look at how your increased versatility can be applied to the activities you do every day as a manager.

PART FOUR

Situational Implementation

CHAPTER ELEVEN

Maintaining a 2R Perspective

N ow that you're armed with the information and tools you need to become a 2R manager, how do you put them into practice in the daily managerial routine? How do you use your increased versatility to hire the best people, make good decisions, and create an effective working group?

To maximize your 2R capability, you need to put aside preconceived notions about what skill is right for a particular managerial function. As you'll discover, even such Relating-focused tasks as recruiting can benefit from Requiring behaviors, and Requiring responsibilities such as managing poor performers can occasionally benefit from Relating approaches.

If you've absorbed the ideas and practiced the 2R skills up to this point, you'll probably do a good job with most of these managerial tasks. But since you're always going to be pulled toward your dominant R, you'll need to be vigilant about being pulled too far, especially when it involves a task you performed primarily in a Relating or Requiring way when you were a 1R manager.

For every managerial function, there is a 2R perspective from which 2R managers produce excellent work while developing and retaining the best people. In decision making, for instance, this 2R perspective leads you to involve your people and then to decide on the best alternative. The 2R perspective combines specific Relating and Requiring skills to perform each function optimally. While there are many managerial functions, I'm going to concentrate on eight key ones with two goals in mind:

- To communicate the 2R perspective

- To provide managers who have learned to use their second R with ideas on how to maintain the 2R perspective and not slip back into a 1R mentality

RECRUITING

Recruiting has become increasingly important as the war for talent heats up and people are expected to work well and independently under relatively light supervision. With the movement toward a service economy, hiring high-quality people becomes even more imperative. Every service business rises and falls on the quality of its people. Yet in most organizations, the recruiting function is regarded as one of many "staff" functions that anyone can do well. Sadly, most firms and managers do *not* do it well, even though it is the most important factor affecting how much time managers spend in training, resolving conflicts, handling underperforming or marginal people, reducing unwanted turnover, rehiring, retraining, and—most important—assuring quality.

For many positions, a good recruiter is one part salesman (developing rapport and presenting opportunities), two parts listener (eliciting information), and two parts appraiser (judging how well the applicant will do in the organization). If this sounds like a mix of Requiring and Relating skills, it is.

2R managers have learned to use their less natural R when necessary in the recruiting process. 2R Relaters (that is, Relaters who become 2R managers) know when to spell out exactly what they need from an applicant; they are not reluctant to communicate that a company expects great things from its people or that a steep learning curve must be climbed if the prospective employee is going to be successful. Similarly, 2R Requirers (Requirers who become 2R managers) know when to listen for insights into a recruit's character, not only to determine if this person is right but also to learn what may be needed to entice him to join.

As you might imagine, some managers talk when they should listen. Others don't probe deeply when they get a clue to a possible problem. Let's explore how 2R managers might slip into 1R thinking during the recruiting process.

2R Relaters may err on the side of wanting to like the applicant versus trying to appraise how well she will function in the organization. For instance, they might become overly focused on appraising how well someone will fit in with the team, overlooking how much the applicant will contribute to getting great work done. They may also be reluctant to state negatives about the job or may fail to set realistic expectations. While 2R Relaters certainly listen to applicants as part of their recruiting responsibilities, they may not listen critically, screening out information that suggests they should probe about a past job experience or ask a difficult question.

Michael was a veteran manager with a large organization, and he was searching for someone to replace his valued assistant of a dozen years, who had left to join another company. He was desperate to replace her and was relieved when he had found the perfect candidate. The applicant was highly organized—one of the criteria for the job— and had the right mix of experience. During their general discussion, the applicant mentioned he had left his previous employer because they "had a falling out." When he said those words, he grimaced and shook his head slightly. Michael, because of his Relating bent, picked up on these cues. He did not, however, ask any follow-up questions, sensing that the applicant didn't want to elaborate. Michael's "sensitivity" served the applicant at the expense of the organization.

2R Requirers are great at defining job specifications and at clarifying exactly what will be needed of the person who fills the job. They are often forceful salespeople, terrific at describing the position accurately and enthusiastically. Where they may run into trouble is in not establishing rapport: talking too much, listening too little, or trying to judge the candidate's suitability too quickly. They cannot learn about the applicant if they are doing the talking, and they cannot be good judges if they haven't been listening. They are likely to tell applicants what they are looking for rather than asking questions to determine whether the applicant fills the bill.

To help assess your own recruiting behavior, read the following scenario, and then think about your response.

Your interview with a candidate, Jerry, is going well, and it's clear that he's done some research about your organization, mentioning a number of facts and figures. Though you believe he's a qualified candidate and has demonstrated his interest through research, Jerry has gotten some of his facts wrong. The glaring one was talking about the company's manufacturing facility in Mexico, which is actually in Honduras. You want to say something to him about his errors, but you don't want to offend him or make him feel that you're overly critical.

Stop now and consider your likely reaction. If you're a Relater, what would you do? If you're a Requirer, what would you do? How would the 2R manager handle it?

Your only purpose is to assess if Jerry is a good candidate and whether you want him to join your firm. He has done some research, which is a positive sign, but since he's made some mistakes, you need to know how he will respond when his errors are pointed out. How will he react to being coached? Defensively? Gratefully? This is an opportunity for you to learn something important. So it's imperative to ask a question to learn more. You might say, "It's clear you have done some reading about us. What did you do to prepare for this interview?" Then, after listening, you might say, "I noticed a few times that you got some facts wrong—for example, the location of our Central American facility. Why do you think that happened?" It is possible that Jerry will handle his response beautifully, increasing the likelihood of your making him an offer. On the other hand, he might try to cover himself, blowing his chances for a job. The point is that the mistakes give you an opportunity to learn more about the applicant.

Many Relaters would not question the errors and would give Jerry the benefit of the doubt for doing research. Many Requirers would reject the applicant without giving him a chance to respond. By not giving the applicant a chance to address errors, Requirers might miss the opportunity to learn more as well as to communicate the high value the company places on accuracy and quality.

CREATING A GOOD WORKING ENVIRONMENT

This function may not be listed in business textbooks, but is absolutely essential for managers in all organizations and at all levels. How well a group functions as a group depends to a large extent on the type of environment the manager creates. Within the limits of the larger organizational culture, the manager sets the climate for his group by his communication skills. Three types of activities are key to his success:

- Welcoming new members
- Clarifying mission and goals (repeating and explaining them more than once)
- Sharing information

Let's look at each in turn.

2R managers attend personally (with help from others) to the details of welcoming new employees. These include welcoming notes before the start date, a plan for the new hire's first day (including who will do the introductions and take her to lunch), having the desk and nameplate ready, inclusion on all mailing lists, and a personal welcome from the manager. These actions are more than cosmetic. They convey that you value the employee even before she has contributed anything. At the end of her first day, when she calls friends and relatives, it's important for her to say, "They really made me feel part of the group."

2R managers clarify the mission and goals, repeating them from the interview process. If the new employee knows how important quality is from day one, the company is much more likely to receive a quality effort from him.

The most important action managers can take to have people feel like a team working for common goals is to *share more information than you have to, all the time.* Nothing fosters a feeling of inclusion more than a manager who shares information as soon as it comes to her or asking for employees' opinions on something she is working on. A 2R manager views any joint travel time as an opportunity to share information. I know how simple "sharing information" reads. But the sad fact is that this easy, highly effective approach to creating a good working environment is not regularly used.

2R Relaters find it very natural to welcome and to share; they probably slip into 1R thinking only when attempting to communicate the team's mission and goals. Relaters tend to dislike repeating the mission statements from the recruiting process, feeling as if they're "demanding" too much too soon. They need to fight their natural inclination to be a member of the team rather than its leader.

2R Requirers need to give attention to the welcoming process to make sure it gets done. Being busy or out of town does not excuse the manager from making sure that someone in the group performs these activities. Of course, once back in the office, the manager should arrange to welcome the new employee as the first item on the agenda. 2R Requirers are most likely to revert to 1R thinking in the areas of sharing information and allowing employees to be parts of solutions to problems the group faces.

DELEGATING

Almost every manager has some issues about delegating. Delegating is a risk-taking venture. If she delegates and doesn't retain some control, she risks not getting the job done to her satisfaction. If she controls it tightly to ensure that it's done the way she wants, she risks not getting ideas that would have made it better, as well as blocking the growth and development of her people. To delegate well, managers must find a way to trust others (Relating) yet maintain some control over the quality of work being produced (Requiring). There are a number of relevant factors to delegating effectively, beginning with the nature of the project. What skills will be needed? How experienced is the person you want to do the task? When you have delegated tasks to this person in the past, how has he done? Who else will need to be involved?

Let's assume you've chosen the right person for the job. The major issue then is how to communicate at the start of the delegation process. If this is done well, the project is much more likely to succeed.

2R managers whose natural style is Relating have two problems to avoid: being too vague about what they want at the start (not asserting) and not following up to see that everything is going well (not ensuring and, if needed, Requiring). They can overcome these problems by making sure they clarify exactly what is to be done, the intended outcome of the task or project, the time frame, who else should be involved, who needs to be coordinated with, and how far the task should be taken before discussing it again. This clarification starts the project in a way that makes it easier for the manager to stay involved. The built-in checkpoints don't allow the Relating manager to delegate and be done with it.

2R managers whose natural style is Requiring must monitor their tendency to control. They want to maintain control even while they delegate. Fortunately, they find it relatively easy to specify all the items mentioned in the preceding paragraph. Instead of focusing their time and energy on hovering over a direct report, they need to address how far the task should be taken before discussing it again. They may want to state explicitly to a direct report that they don't want to overcontrol and will depend on him for frequent status reports. Secure in the knowledge that the project has preplanned review points, the Requiring manager can relax and allow work to proceed without constantly checking up on the person doing the job.

MANAGING EXPECTATIONS

If you just drove from the suburbs to the city and it took forty minutes, you might be delighted because you expected it to take an hour. Or you might be furious because you thought it would only take twenty minutes at this time of the day. The trip took forty minutes in both scenarios; the difference in outcomes depends on your expectations.

To a significant extent, expectations determine job satisfaction. While what actually happens on the job obviously has an impact, expectations play a larger role than most people think. Employees leave firms when their expectations haven't been met, which is one good reason 2R managers create appropriate expectations. Overselling on the front end (in the recruiting stage) risks disappointment later. Underselling risks failing to attract the employee. Expectations need to be both attractive and realistic to ensure long-term satisfaction.

I once worked with Brian, a Requiring manager of about fifty people he wanted to motivate to perform well. Brian explained to his people that since he "paid for performance," all of his direct reports would be eligible for raises up to 20 percent annually (this was when inflation was running at an annual rate of 12 percent). What do you think happened when the highest-performing person received a 17 percent raise? Everyone was angry. Even the best performer asked what she would have had to do to get the other 3 percent. Without the expectations Brian created, a 17 percent increase would have been highly satisfying.

Expectations must be managed early to head off misunderstandings. When a manager knows that one of her people is expecting a promotion he's not going to receive, she needs to address this issue sooner rather than later. She might say, "I just heard you say that you were expecting a promotion by the end of the year. While I think you are doing well and are on track for a promotion, I don't think it will happen that soon, and I don't want you to be disappointed." He won't love to hear this, but he'd much prefer hearing it now than closer to the end of the year. The longer someone expects something that doesn't happen, the greater the disappointment. Managers need to risk a small sting early to avoid a big pain later.

2R Relaters need to be on guard against reverting to the old "leave people happy" strategy for ending each interaction. Being completely honest as much as possible is the course they should follow, as opposed to spinning information in a way that raises expectations. Not only does spinning consume a lot of energy, but the ploy is usually seen through very quickly. 2R Relaters need to remind themselves that their people don't expect everything to go well all the time and prefer that their bosses tell them the truth.

2R Requirers need to remain sensitive to their direct reports' expectations. If they oversell, they may not be aware that they made certain promises or that a direct report is disappointed. They might also undersell by being very clear about the negatives but failing to be sensitive to their people's need for assignments that have a payoff. Painting a task as a terrible burden creates a different type of expectation, but one that's equally destructive. 2R Requirers need to be careful when dashing someone's expectations, remembering that it's much more important to the employee than they might think it should be. Curbing expectations is a difficult part of any manager's job, but 2R managers learn how to cushion the blow by showing some empathy when doing so.

Do you raise or dampen expectations in ways that have a long-term negative impact on your people? Consider the following "expectation practices" that result from versatility backsliding, and determine the ones to which you are susceptible:

- Painting an unfairly optimistic picture of a prospective position during a job interview

- Reassuring a direct report when he receives a negative performance review with "next time you'll do better"

- Failing to tell your people about the extent of the organization's troubles because you don't want to scare them about possible cutbacks

- Pointing out all the negatives of a job so that your direct reports won't be able to accuse you of "sugar-coating" unpleasant realities

- Allowing a direct report's expectations to build even though you know there's little hope they'll be realized in pay, promotions, transfers, project management opportunities, or other areas
- Destroying someone's expectations about a promotion, raise, or transfer with a quick, matter-of-fact statement

DECISION MAKING

Requiring managers (even 2R Requirers) tend to assemble information quickly because they feel an urgency to make decisions that will get things accomplished. While this trait can be beneficial, it can also result in premature decisions and a lack of participation from others.

Donna was a highly successful manager for a well-known financial services company. Her people knew that once she made up her mind, she rarely changed it. She received feedback about this trait and was making progress involving others and allowing their comments to influence her decisions before they became set in stone. Under pressure however, she reverted to her former style. When she struggled with the slowness of participatory decision making, she might blurt out her favorite expression, "Cut to the chase."

2R Requiring managers who maintain their versatility recognize that the antidote to this reflex is to stay open longer. As soon as you decide something, you stop being able to hear new information objectively. If new information conflicts with the decision, it is discounted or ignored. If it aligns with the decision, it is remembered and used to convince others. The media, unfortunately, reinforce our impulse to decide quickly. Their opinion polls, for instance, suggest that it's possible to provide a reasonable answer even when we don't have sufficient information on which to base an opinion. In addition, we're constantly listening to people on the news and talk shows make snap judgments when it's clear that they have incomplete knowledge about the subject. 2R Requiring managers, especially, need to resist the rush-to-judgment mentality and force themselves to remain open about opposing and unusual ideas before making a decision. Only by allowing others to comment, suggest alternatives, and bring forth problems or perspectives that are different can a manager be a top-flight decision maker.

2R Relating managers tend to be highly participative in decision making. They ask their people to suggest new ideas, offer reactions, and involve other individuals in the decisions to be made. These are all great qualities, but 2R Relating managers should be alert for two decision-making areas in which they're vulnerable.

First, they know from experience that some of their people will dislike any decision. This creates conflict, which makes them uncomfortable. They need to remind themselves that this kind of conflict is normal and expected by their employees.

Second, they have a difficult time making a decision based solely on their own best judgment after consulting with others. It is often easier to go with what the majority of their people think. But their people don't have the responsibility for achieving the group's goals. Only the managers have that responsibility. And they will perform it best by basing decisions on their judgment, after consulting with others, of what will help them achieve the group's objectives, independent of how many people in the group agree. When managers use this criterion, they need not apologize or feel guilty because someone else disagrees with it.

2R managers value both words in the phrase "participative management." They encourage others to participate in deliberations before a decision has been made, resulting in more and better ideas. This manager is not giving away control of the decision. Nor is he waiting for consensus before making it. His advantage as the decision maker is that he has more alternatives to consider. In addition, he has involved the people who will ultimately implement the decision in the process of making it. Even if their opinions weren't supported, they were heard, which makes them feel invested.

Dealing with bad ideas is the challenge of participative management. When people bring a Requiring manager suggestions that she knows will not work, her immediate instinct will be to dismiss them and explain why the ideas won't work. Such an approach can be quite insulting and make employees think twice before volunteering ideas in the future. A 2R alternative would be to ask the person who makes the suggestion, "What problem are you trying to solve with this suggestion?" Most often you will hear a legitimate problem in response, allowing you to say, "I agree that's a problem, but we need to find another solution, because I see some real issues with the specific solution you are suggesting." The key here is to listen for understanding while resisting expressing your judgment until you have heard more about the person's thinking.

2R Relaters, being receptive to ideas and suggestions, are likely to get many they don't think will work well. A Relating manager might even ask the person who proposes a flawed idea to try it out and learn for herself that it isn't viable. This approach can waste valuable time. As an alternative, this Relating manager should consider asking the same question as the Requiring manager ("What problem are you trying to solve with this suggestion?") in order to find other solutions.

The danger of participative management for Relaters is that they have trouble dealing with multiple strong opinions. Not wanting to hurt anyone's feelings, the Relating manager allows the discussion to drag on too long or to become mired in complexities that prevent any clear path from emerging. At some point, good decision makers decide and then take responsibility.

Which of the following best describes your decision-making inclinations?

- "I am most likely to make decisions without much discussion and debate. I decide quickly because we don't have the luxury of time in our business. While I try to gather information and ideas, I'm confident that I know the subjects involved as well as anyone and can rely on my own experience to determine the best course of action."
- "I believe I have a great team and know that the more input I solicit, the better the team's decision will be. My goal is to have everyone on the team 100 percent behind whatever we decide. If that's the case, I can be certain we'll implement the decision with great energy and shared accountability. While it's true that sometimes we have a lot of long meetings before we resolve things, I feel it's important for everyone's voice to be heard."
- "There are times when I need to decide fast, and if that happens, I'm not averse to limiting discussion to a few key points in order to gather the information we need to make the right choice. In other situations, however, I recognize that we have the luxury to do some research and brainstorm different approaches. In these instances, I step back and let my people talk their points through while I play the role of facilitator. Although ultimately I will make the decision, I want a far-reaching discussion to gain the information and ideas I need to make a good decision."

COACHING

Although coaching can be a daily activity to foster short-term learning, our focus here will be coaching for long-term professional growth and identifying tendencies that might block someone from achieving this growth. At some point, a manager sees an obstacle standing in the way of a direct report's development. He's convinced that this person could contribute more if she only knew what the manager knows. At this point, the manager is primed to coach. He becomes the mirror that allows his direct report to see how her behaviors affect others at work. The manager can't change the employee directly, but he can facilitate change by holding up this mirror.

Typically, the mirror translates into feedback. Giving feedback as a coach, however, is difficult for many managers. Too often, manager and direct report are working at cross-purposes: the manager wants to give advice that will change the direct report, and the direct report wants encouragement. To solve this problem, a 2R manager provides honest encouragement but also points out how a specific change can help the direct report be more successful.

Here's a typical coaching opportunity. You have a talented direct report who is a procrastinator, putting things off until it is an emergency, sometimes missing deadlines and always too late for review. You've experienced this issue yourself; it isn't something you're guessing at or just heard from someone else. There are serious business consequences, such as a customer being upset. Unless he can overcome this bad work habit, your direct report's work is unacceptable. To coach effectively, on this subject or any other major issue blocking success, you will need to lead him through the following steps:

1. Understanding the consequences of his problem behavior
2. Wanting to change it (not just seeing it in the mirror, but wanting to change it)
3. Figuring out a plan for change
4. Taking action, getting feedback, and staying the course

To start taking these steps, you might initiate a discussion with an opening sentence like "I've noticed something I think is limiting you and want to talk to you about it." Then name the item in one or two sentences—not more than a minute of monologue here. After that, ask your employee if he knows he behaves in this problematic manner. You must learn early in the conversation if this is a surprise to him or if he's already aware of it. If the latter, you can ask if he knows the consequences of the action or behavior. You are trying to get to the point where you can ask if he wants to work on changing it (step 2). Don't go too fast on step 1—it's important for this person to really want to change. Seeing the consequences can help him maintain his commitment to change. If the problem you are identifying comes as a surprise to him, you will not get too far on the four steps at the first meeting because he hasn't yet accepted that there is a problem. He will want examples. After you give them to him, he may make excuses or try to shift the blame in ways you don't anticipate. You might then say something like, "Since I have observed an issue that you have not seen, let's agree to watch for it in the next few weeks on the assignments you now have." Even though he has not acknowledged he has a problem, he may well do better after this discussion. Some people can't admit faults. If he changes, you don't care if he admits it. If he doesn't change, you can then start step 1 again, this time using the latest example as evidence.

As you can imagine or may have experienced, coaching in this way is not a quick fix. Managers need skill and patience to coach direct reports so that they eventually change their behaviors. Given this coaching environment, managers with Relating and Requiring tendencies can easily make mistakes.

Requiring managers would generally like to coach as follows: "I'll tell you what you need to do differently, and from now on, you should do it that way! It should be a two step process—step 1 and step 4." Certainly, eliminating steps 2 and 3 would make the process simpler—no need to check for understanding, no need to gain commitment to change, no need to help people define exactly what they need to do differently, and no need for continuous monitoring and occasional interventions. As tempting as these shortcuts might be for Requiring managers, they won't work. 2R Requirers must slow down and recognize that each of the four steps is needed for real change to occur and that their job is to help their people through all of them. Although Requirers have a relatively easy time identifying the problem and asking the employee to identify the consequences, they are often not skilled in helping their employee know what they must do to make the change. They may need assistance from their boss, from their library, or from the human resource department to suggest ideas for how to make the change. 2R Requirers need to have the patience to provide feedback if the employee slips back into the old behavior and use compliments when they see positive change.

Relating managers have problems coaching because they know that part of this process involves addressing an individual's weakness and sometimes results in embarrassment or conflict. Relaters instinctively want to avoid the discomfort caused by confronting a direct report about problematic behavior. As a result, they get bogged down when it comes to getting started with coaching, staying focused on coaching for change (rather than becoming sidetracked on what the employee is good at), and persevering through all the backsliding in performance.

2R Relaters must shift their thinking if they want to coach effectively. Specifically, they should stop viewing the coaching process as a confrontation and start seeing it as a way to help a direct report grow. This shift in thinking can help them overcome their natural aversion to conflict. If they don't give their employees the gift of information needed to grow, who will?

2R Relaters must guard against their tendency to backpedal when they describe the individual's problem and its negative consequences. Accepting that the employee needs to hear the problem and feel the consequences before wanting to change is crucial. 2R Relaters practice what they want to say the night before the first meeting, distilling their message to one or two sentences. They also avoid guessing or brooding about how their direct report will react. If they dwell on an anticipated reaction, their natural empathy will get in the way of coaching.

Managers with Relating tendencies automatically want to make a direct report feel better if the individual doesn't agree with or understand their assessment. 2R managers guard against this tendency, understanding that when they encounter resistance or anger, they have not failed at the process but are only on step 1 (identifying the problem). All they can do initially is hold up the mirror. After that, the employee has to engage in the process.

PERFORMANCE MANAGEMENT

Over six months or a year, how does a manager appraise performance against preset goals or predefined criteria and then provide feedback to the employee? This function used to be called performance appraisal and is now most commonly called performance management.

There is plenty of literature on performance management, most of it devoted to how hard it is to do this function well. Rather than summarize these lessons, I'd like to focus exclusively on providing a 2R perspective on the function, along with some comments on how 2R managers can maintain their versatility.

Performance management is a process that is used for several purposes—development (helping the employee grow in the future), determining pay, and assessing career paths. These issues are all vitally important to the employee. Yet they are based on some type of subjective measuring approach or process. Every performance management system has its strengths and weaknesses, but all rely on the judgment of the manager. Managers need to be as fair and objective as possible when deciding these issues, as well as caring and sensitive when discussing their conclusions with the employee. If the employee perceives the process to be fair, you are a long way toward retaining the employee in your group. It is a great opportunity to build trust (or conversely, an opportunity to lose it).

In the appraisal function, try to appreciate all the kinds of contributions each employee makes, especially ones you do not have or are weak in. The broader the perspective you bring to this appraisal, the fairer you will be in how-to-do-better-in-the-future meetings; you'll do a much better job identifying future career paths and making pay decisions.

If you do not have all the information necessary to make a fair appraisal (for example, if some of your people work with others outside your department far more than they work with you), find ways to get it. Don't wing it or complete the appraisal forms by guessing.

In the feedback process, try to identify major themes of development for the employee. Avoid telling the employee about every little thing that annoys you. Stick to the big stuff. Going beyond one, two, or possibly three themes will strain the employee's ability to assimilate the feedback.

If your organization's policy is for you to go over all the ratings you submitted, you will have to defend your appraisals. Do so in a way that communicates that your appraisal represents your judgment at one particular point in time. Don't be rigid in your defense. You may not have had all the information or been right on each minor assessment factor.

In the feedback process, maintain a positive, future orientation to your comments. You are trying to help the employee do well or do better in the future. "Here's what I'd like to see you work on in the next six months" (as opposed to a tone that conveys "Here's where you went wrong last month. Don't do it again").

You should also allow time to listen as well as talk. Even if you disagree, it's important for the employee to be able to defend herself, give you more information than you might have had, and voice her own thoughts and reactions. You do not have to win every argument with the employee. Keep your eye on the goal—having her hear the major things she should work on to make a greater contribution in the future.

Finally, separate the pay and performance meetings. Reviewing performance should be first. This meeting is to let the employee know how he is doing and how he can do better in the future. In addition, you might learn something that influences your pay decision. Employees cannot concentrate on the performance discussion if they know a pay discussion will immediately follow. If you cover pay first, they will react to that message and not hear the performance message. For this reason, pay discussions should be a week or more later. Make these discussions short, and be sure the pay decision reflects the previous performance discussion.

Obviously, there are numerous opportunities for mishandling employees in appraising and providing feedback about performance. When done effectively, however, direct reports are tremendously impressed with managers who demonstrate seriousness and fairness. To achieve this, 2R managers with Relating or Requiring tendencies need to be especially vigilant against slipping back into 1R thinking as they assess their people and provide feedback.

For example, several psychological factors may lead 2R Relaters to give a lot of "good" ratings to mediocre performers, including these:

- Knowing they will be meeting with the employee to defend their ratings (a confrontation risk)

- Feeling they lack definitive information and not wanting to make a mistake with such a personal and important decision for the employee

- Being in the habit of giving employees the benefit of the doubt

- Wanting to like the employee and be liked in return

Relaters are strongly compelled to shade ratings upward, and it would be misleading to state that mere awareness of this tendency will completely eliminate it. However, 2R Relaters can take two performance management actions to maintain 2R behaviors. First, they develop their ability to appraise people critically. There is always a tendency to be blind to weaknesses. When Relating managers are asked to write some paragraphs about an employee's performance, their paragraphs are often brief and general. It is hard for them to come up with fine distinctions in the performance of their people. (For example, is a direct report argumentative, assertive, or aggressive? Shallow, unimaginative, or shy? Manipulative or competitive?)

Second, 2R Relaters must stay honest with themselves. When they're certain a direct report has delivered a mediocre (or worse) performance, they don't let sympathy override their best judgment. Valuing their own judgment enough to make decisions based on it, they're prepared to defend it with their direct reports.

Though the feedback discussions will still be uncomfortable for most 2R Relaters, they should be aware that if they minimize the negatives (missing opportunities to coach for better performance) and only praise the positives, most of their praise will be discounted by their people. The major question for the 2R Relater to ask after a performance discussion is "Was I honest and forthcoming with my best judgment?" If the answer is yes, long-term trust will flourish.

Requirers look forward to the performance management part of their jobs. The process can help them be clearer about what they want from an employee. At the same time, they may not realize they are at risk of losing or destroying trust. The tendency to view this as a task (to be completed quickly so that they can get back to work) and the possible insensitivity to the intensely personal nature of performance discussions can cause Requiring managers trouble.

To avoid this trouble, 2R Requirers learn to look for and appreciate all the positive contributions employees are making. They come to appreciate traits that help the group bond and work together effectively. These managers also develop sufficient sensitivity to how their people view the process, going through it in a thorough, serious, and careful manner.

The major questions for the 2R Requirer to ask after a performance discussion are "Did I take my time and show (with my tone of voice and expression) that I understand how important the discussion is?" and "Did I communicate that I appreciate the positive contributions this employee makes?" If the answers are yes, the job will have been well done.

MANAGING POOR AND MARGINAL PERFORMERS

All poor performances must be confronted, not just because one individual is not doing his job but because your entire group desperately needs you to deal with this problem. Negative consequences spread if they are not eliminated. Obviously, this is a Requiring skill. 2R Relaters will try to ask first for change and then assert and clarify that changes must be made. When the employee doesn't respond to these attempts, the manager must be very direct: "If you do not improve significantly, starting today, I will have to ask you to leave." The easiest way for 2R Relaters to stay strong in this process is to remember that a poor performer is hurting everyone in the group. 2R Requirers, on the other hand, can rely on their natural style to deal with poor performers, but they still need to remember to treat people with dignity and to approach a termination with grace rather than anger.

What confuses some managers of both Relating and Requiring tendencies is when performance is good but behavior is bad (rude, sexist, demeaning, bullying, or the like). Although some companies tolerate bad behavior for the sake of performance, I would suggest that the damage you don't see exceeds what's visible. Whatever bad behavior you're witnessing is only the tip of the iceberg: the rude or obnoxious employee is likely creating significant fallout by hurting the company's relationship with vendors and customers, creating internal tensions, and diverting energy that could be applied to work.

Requiring managers may be inclined to give behavioral transgressions a pass when the work is good. Relating managers won't share this inclination but aren't eager to engage in a confrontation. Both types of managers tend to wait too long before telling the employee to stop the offending behavior, that it is a serious issue. 2R managers have seen the positive results of dealing with these issues and understand that their people will respect their efforts to provide an environment that protects them from bad behavior.

Finally, let's turn to marginal performance, which differs from poor performance in that the former involves occasional good performance or effort. Typically, marginal performers engender hope in their managers—especially Relating managers—that they can do the job decently, even if they are not yet working at a satisfactory level. In many instances, they are inconsistent performers, doing a good job one day or one week and a poor one the next.

2R Relaters need to watch their tendency to cut marginal employees too much slack, allowing their work to remain marginal in the vain hope that they will become more consistent. 2R Requirers need to be careful not to jump the gun and jettison mediocre performers who might be able to improve their results with some strong coaching and direction. To guard against these tendencies, managers should ask themselves the following question: "Is this person not performing because he lacks the ability, the will, or the training to do this job?"

If someone lacks the ability but is making a real effort to meet your standards, you should consider transferring him to a more suitable position. If you contact the HR department to check about such a transfer and nothing is available, then you need to seek an amicable parting. When an individual lacks the training to do the job but has the capability and the will, you should help him get the training. If lack of will is the problem, tell the person goodbye, even if she has the ability. Someone who doesn't care enough to perform well is not a reliable employee.

Managers cannot achieve their goals and objectives with marginal or poor performers. When 2R managers are trying to decide what to do with problem people, they ask themselves, "What action will best help the rest of my group achieve?"

CHAPTER TWELVE

Getting Started

To change your management style, you may need a push. In the real world, a boss or coach could give you that push via feedback about how you are doing as a manager. Negative feedback would identify where you're falling short of 2R performance and provide the motivation to make some changes. Positive feedback would also motivate you, giving you a sense of what you might achieve if you could master both Rs. Though it's not possible for this book to provide feedback to you directly, it can do so indirectly. First, though, I'd like to explain why I feel so strongly about how this feedback can get you started on a 2R path.

I became a more effective manager because of the feedback I received. In Chapter Nine, I provided a glimpse of what that feedback involved. Let me go into a bit more detail here. Over a number of years, the people I worked with had given me an accurate profile of my managing style. On the Relating side, I asked questions easily, listened for understanding, cared what people said, and was influenced by it, but I did all this from a problem-solving, task orientation rather than a desire to relate better. I was weak on complimenting and encouraging behaviors; though friendly, I was emotionally aloof. On the

Requiring side, I set high standards and had high expectations, saw the potential in my people, and was forthright in explaining how they could reach it. At the same time, I was slow to see the need for, and resistant to, Requiring behaviors. In 2R terms, I was a 2R Requirer who asserted easily but struggled to require when needed, who listened well but struggled to compliment and encourage.

When I began to incorporate this feedback, I slowed down my pace, took more time with people, and made an active effort to communicate to my reports the things they were doing well. As I changed my style, I could see the impact on their faces. Not expecting compliments from me, they beamed when I recognized and acknowledged their contributions. Only then understanding how much my compliments meant to them, I was surprised at their subsequent renewed energy and motivation.

Direct feedback like this can make quite an impact. It can stimulate you to ask yourself some key questions that may result in a new direction for your career, or it can tell you where to direct your next efforts to reach your potential as a manager. When people you work with are willing to level with you about your impact as a manager, they are giving you a great gift. I hope you will solicit regular feedback from your group and your boss and be open to their words. Until then, I'd like to provide the next best thing: I'm going to talk to you directly, as if I were your personal coach. Though I obviously don't know you— you each have unique issues and personalities—you're either a natural Relater or a natural Requirer. Furthermore, you fall into or near the nine managerial types discussed throughout the book.

I'm going to address each of you as if you're sitting across from me, discussing what you should be considering and how to get started toward maximizing your happiness and your contributions to your organization. While only one of the nine types is relevant to you, I'd encourage you to read the other types for perspectives and approaches that will be useful with your direct reports and the people you report to.

THE ABDICATOR

Why do you want to be a manager? The answer to this question will tell us how to proceed. If you feel that you will earn more money, then we should explore if that assumption is true. In many companies, an abdicator manager will not make more money than a good individual contributor with needed expertise. If the title and the prestige of the role have been paramount, I would argue that if you continue to abdicate, you won't have them for very long.

I'm asking you to confront this issue because as an abdicator, you're not putting your heart and soul into managing. Though you have a natural managerial style, you're not using it. It may be that you don't really want to be a manager. It could be that you're just going through a difficult personal or professional period in your life and are distracted from the job of managing. Most likely, however, you enjoy the direct contribution part of your job so much that the managing part always takes a lower priority. Whatever the reason, you're in an untenable position. As a manager, you have been given a great deal of responsibility but have not yet accepted it. Over time, this is emotionally and physically draining and literally unhealthy. I urge you to decide if you really want to be a manager.

If, after serious reflection, you decide you do want to continue to manage, return to the survey in Chapter Two and note all the items you scored 1 or 2. Create an action plan designed to increase the regularity with which you perform a given behavior. Pick your more natural behaviors first. Use Chapters Four and Eight if you are a Relater and Chapters Three and Nine if you are a Requirer. After three to six months of trying to be more consistent in these behaviors, ask yourself if you like the changes you're making. Do you feel you are on the right track and want to continue to grow as a manager? If you do, terrific. You're becoming a better manager and a new management type (either a friend or a supervisor). At some point down the road, you can then go for your second R or accept your status as a 1R manager.

If you dislike your new behaviors, find them difficult, or just prefer to spend all your time doing what you like best, you might consider becoming an individual contributor. Don't feel as if you're "stepping down." In reality, you're stepping into a role that better suits your skills and personality. Pretending to possess skills you lack or acting like you enjoy being a manager when you don't serves no one well, neither your employees nor yourself. Give the idea of a trial period some thought as you attempt to find the role best suited to the organization's needs and your own happiness.

THE FRIEND

Are you still comfortable continuing to be only a friend, knowing that your people want and need you to be more? You know the trade-offs—is being liked worth all the compromises you're making? I know that there have been times you've protected people on your team who didn't deserve it; they've taken advantage of your avuncular attitude by slacking off on assignments and taking days off when you really needed them to be working. As I hope you know by now, your friendly approach is preventing your people from reaching their full potential and doing the highest-quality work.

If you're willing to endure some personal discomfort, make a commitment to develop your other R and start learning to assert yourself. In the long run, you'll be helping yourself, your company, and your employees more, but to do so, you're going to have to deal with conflicts and disagreements you avoided in the past. I would urge you to make this trade-off not just to become a better manager but also so you can achieve more of what you want and deserve personally. By being more assertive, you'll improve long-term relationships with everyone in your life.

Begin by reviewing some of the following versatility-fostering beliefs you want to work on:

- My reports cannot grow without the feedback about what they are not doing well or could do better.
- Poor performance puts extra burdens on my group and on me.
- My employees expect me to manage, make decisions, set priorities, and deal with unacceptable behavior; the conflicts this creates are necessary.
- Asking for what I need and want is not demanding behavior; it is normal managing behavior.

Pick the one that has the greatest current relevance. For example, let's assume that when you read the words "deal with unacceptable behavior" in the third bulleted item, Hank jumped into your mind. His behaviors have been irritating you (and some others in your group) for months.

Begin asserting by telling Hank what is on your mind, how you react when he behaves badly, and what you expect from him. By focusing on one individual, you narrow and define your course of action. Once you've been successful asserting with one individual (success might be change, or it might be that Hank leaves your employ), expand your effort to include more versatility-fostering beliefs and more people. Go through the 4M Plan as suggested in Chapter

Eight to test how comfortable you can become while asserting; then evaluate the results. Remember, it took you years to become a friend, so you should not expect that you're going to become a 2R manager overnight. By the end of the four months, you should see and feel some significant progress and know if you are on the right course for your growth.

Keep in mind that the payoff for enduring some of the discomfort is that you're going to get more of what you want just by asking for it. To this point, you've been shortchanging yourself, settling for less than you are capable of achieving. When you learn to ask for what you want, you'll find that you can achieve far more than you did in the past, and perhaps far more than you dreamed.

THE PLEASER

The same question I would ask an abdicator also applies here: Are you sure you want to be a manager? To do a good job, you must confront people, set priorities, decide things that others disagree with, ask for what you need, and deal with the resulting conflicts. Your current style is to avoid "unpleasantness." You may even have gone so far as to take the blame for others' failures rather than confront people you know have been slacking off. If you find this basic and essential managerial function difficult, why do you want to be a manager? I'm not saying this to be mean but to help you clarify what it is you are trying to achieve.

You might answer that you love having many relationships in which you can help people. Perhaps you love to teach people what you know. In that case, we might explore how you can best help your people. Moving from being a pleaser to being a friend is the first step. By making this relatively small change, you'll reduce your relating behaviors to an appropriate level. You're not helping your direct reports by appeasing them. Like a parent who is fearful of making a child angry, you either don't set any limits or don't enforce the limits you set.

The first step toward being a friend is to stop yourself from all the guessing about how others feel and worrying about reactions to your actions. If people don't like something, they can speak for themselves. You do not have to spend so much time trying to get inside the heads of the people who work for you. Spend the time working on your individual tasks. Use as many ideas as you can from Chapter Four to reduce the over-Relating. How your day goes is no longer dependent on what reactions, readings, clues, or vibes you pick up from your people because you aren't trying to pick them up anymore. If you can do that for two weeks, I can almost guarantee two things: your reports will like you more, and they will come to you instead of you going to them. Try it. There's virtually no risk.

Obviously, over the longer term, you will need to learn how to assert yourself more. But this can come after you have created a little more independence from your direct reports. Look around, and you'll see Requiring managers in your organization who have strong relationships with their people. Invariably, these managers told their employees things that they didn't want to hear but that helped them develop. Be aware that these strong relationships are possible even when managers don't relate as much as you do or when they don't relate much at all. Reread the versatility-fostering beliefs; then practice asserting behaviors. Repeat to yourself that not every interaction with your direct reports has to end with everyone feeling good. When you leave a meeting or discussion where you know your direct report is upset or angry, remind yourself that this negative emotion can be a catalyst for a positive outcome. Sometimes it takes getting angry to deal with certain issues.

Don't expect an easy journey to 2R manager status. Since you need to be liked, your aversion to asserting isn't just going to disappear. If you need motivation to take this tough path, however, remind yourself that you're in a wonderful position to make a difference in the lives and careers of your people. You can help them reach their potential and in the process have a long-term relationship, not just a short-term sense of comfort. As they hear some straight talk from you, they're going to produce better results that boost their careers. That's the opportunity you now have as a manager.

THE SUPERVISOR

You are doing a very respectable job and may feel you are ready for a promotion. Since I think that is not likely to happen, we need to talk about it. Certainly you're effective as a first-line manager, because you do well supervising repetitive tasks and familiar processes and outcomes. You give clear instructions, meet deadlines, and in terms of fundamental managerial responsibilities are a competent manager.

Your lack of Relating skills, however, stands in the way of higher-level managerial positions. Your people don't feel you either know them as individuals or are interested in their ideas. They don't believe you care about or are doing much to facilitate their careers. As a result, your boss has been very selective in the projects she assigns you, withholding those involving unfamiliar subjects. Basically, she is deciding that you cannot do activities such as brainstorming or working with teams to develop new solutions, so she gives you assignments she knows you can handle. This may contribute to your sense that you are ready for a promotion, but clearly, your boss is limiting your growth, based on the Relating skills she has seen from you so far.

If you're willing to work on your Relating skills and are serious about wanting a higher-level management job, you need to force yourself to listen, withhold judgment, ask questions, and involve and nurture others. I realize that's a tall order. Here's where you can start. Pick one of the following versatility-fostering beliefs that you want to work on:

- My employees know things I don't about how best to get the job done.
- My employees may have new ideas about how to do a better job.
- I would make better decisions if I consulted with my employees and gave them a chance to react to my ideas or tentative conclusions.
- My employees need to feel appreciated to do their best work.

Let's assume that you have a current decision to make and would like to try involving your people more in the process. Make sure you have not concluded yet and are not using others' involvement to maneuver toward the conclusion you have already reached. Design a process whereby you ask others to help you think through the alternatives and the considerations of each. When you have completed this process, you may well be surprised at how many good ideas your people have provided.

Perhaps you will then be open to adopting a few more of the versatility-fostering beliefs. As you loosen the controls and allow others to participate, you should see several of your people respond very favorably. Some of them will surprise you with ideas they were hiding. As they open up and share these with you, be sure to compliment them and encourage them to bring more ideas. You will be on your way toward getting more help to do excellent work in the group and in the process showing that you can accept assignments that are more challenging.

THE DEMANDER

I know that you have high standards and want to produce the best work possible. In trying to do so, you've probably felt that your people let you down. Either they can't produce the quality you want, or they don't have the commitment to do whatever it takes. They never seem to be good enough for you. Whenever one leaves, you aren't upset, as it gives you a chance to hire a "better" person. But you have chased away some good people. You're so obsessed with turning out great work that you don't realize the price such an obsession is exacting. Though your group has done a terrific job on some projects, many of the people who contributed have transferred elsewhere or have left the company. And there have been times when your group hasn't come through with great results. I think an objective observer would say that your people have learned that you want to do things your way, so they wait to hear what your way is. They don't take the natural initiative they once did.

You may try to defend yourself by saying that you were trained to demand the best from people and that the company has always put results above everything else. There's no question that the organization has always prized your ability to deliver high-quality results on time. You were promoted to your current position because of these attributes. The problem is that you're not consistently getting good performance from your people. Not everyone is like you, and not everyone is going to respond well to your "results at all costs" tactics. Setting the bar high is fine most of the time, but you also need to recognize that some situations call for supplemental approaches to encourage performing to your exacting standards.

Begin by incorporating as many of the lighten-up exercises in Chapter Three as you can. Reducing the excessiveness in your controlling behavior is the right starting point. Then look for ways you can appreciate someone else's ideas or suggestions. Others must feel that they can help and that you will not interrupt, correct, or modify their ideas without giving them credit. You have people in your group who are intimidated to the point that their self-esteem suffers. Help them feel better about their work and capabilities. Look for something good to compliment them on. Say, " I like that! That's a good idea, thanks." If you can do this for the next month, you will see how much your recognition spurs people to give you more good ideas. If they come up with a bad idea, ask them (in a kind tone of voice) what problem they are trying to solve with the idea and then find the common ground by agreeing on the problem. After the first month, you may find it easier to solicit other people's ideas and allow them to contribute. You may want to invite greater participation from your people. By helping your direct reports feel valued as contributing members of the team rather than "worker bees" who follow your orders, you'll motivate them to work harder and more creatively. The measure that motivates you is high-quality work, and I want you to realize that there is more than one way of getting your people to produce it.

Also, I need to say that if you cannot improve in this area, we will clearly not add more people to your group and may need to reduce the number of people you manage to the ones who can take your demanding style. I have worked with other demanders who made the commitment to become energizers by lightening up on their requiring as they were learning how to relate better. They became extremely valuable and effective managers.

THE ENCROACHER

Because you're able to both relate and require, you have great potential as a manager. You move quickly and are at ease with people and get a lot done. However, you won't realize this potential until you stop doing things that hurt you. You take your natural Relating strength to an extreme, trying too hard to meet your needs to be close to your people. Some of them pull back from you in order to retain their privacy. They feel that you're not satisfied if they just do a good job; they have to deal with your frequent phone calls, e-mails, visits, and lunches. You may get offended when they pull back, eat lunch at their desk, or otherwise hint that they need more distance from you. This leads to your reaching out more, which only exacerbates the problem.

You need to be aware that you're locked in to this encroaching cycle in which you try too hard to be close to your people, they resist, and their resistance triggers either a greater Relating response or a Requiring response on your part. The Requiring response is often insistence on the need to be together. When you require that your people see you too often, you are encroaching on their time and space. Your people become unsure if your energies are directed at doing the best work or satisfying your need to be active together.

Backing off and giving people more room are simple actions that will move you in a 2R direction. You should also organize your interactions to avoid making constant calls or trips to a direct report's office. By writing down and consolidating what you absolutely need to talk to each person about, you won't be as vulnerable to frequent encroaching impulses. Schedule your interactions rather than leave them to chance. In addition, capitalize on your natural sensitivity by registering people's cues that they don't want to talk to you. Note warning signals in their voices or discomfort in their body language that communicate that "now is not a good time." Don't be hurt or insulted when you pick up these signals. They're being sent not because people dislike you but because they're busy or they need to focus on increasing their work output or work quality at the moment.

The key to reaching your potential has to do with reducing your need to use Relating to control others. Most people associate control with demanding behavior, but you control through Relating behaviors. Using Relating as your primary tool, you control outcomes by controlling the agenda, the timing, the process. Make sure that your Relating and Requiring are in service of both developing your people and delivering great work rather than a personal need to interact. If you can ease up on your need to control, people will respond better to your Relating actions.

Start by asking yourself a few questions:

- Can I consolidate interactions with my people so that I don't interrupt them as much?
- Can I play "Stretch It Out," going a longer and longer time between interactions?
- Are there some agreements I could get that would help me relax on my need to initiate conversations because I would feel assured people will talk to me when they need to?
- Are there any other ways to give them more autonomy or control of the timing or length of our interactions?

As you find the answers and put them into practice, your style will be much closer to that of a 2R manager.

THE ENERGIZER

Every organization needs its energizers—managers who thirst for results and have the skills to get them. The key question is whether you are keeping your best people with you or pushing them away. While you have all the requisite skills to relate and require, they may not be in the right proportions yet to maximize your success and effectiveness.

You are capable of talking to direct reports in such an inspiring way that they'd run through a wall for you. Sometimes, however, your energizing approach goes over the top. Your people come away feeling they've been subjected to your motivational techniques to the point of exhaustion. With the best of intentions, you sometimes make people feel they're going to have to work night and day to achieve your dream. The greater the energy you attempt to impart, the harder it is to sustain. Some people would respond better to simple conversations or a low-key approach.

Your habitual speed of action may result in not giving others a chance to input to the process or some things not getting done as thoroughly as they should. Either situation leaves a wake of dissatisfaction that can fester if left unattended. Your people need to participate in the decisions and outcomes and be appreciated for their contributions. You're a leader but should not be too far ahead of them without the proper connection.

I suspect that you seek to energize in order to gain a measure of control over outcomes. You assume that if you can get people's internal flames to burn hotter, they'll work that much harder and faster. Recognize, though, that they can also burn out. I'd like you to make a conscious effort to vary your style depending on the individual and the situation. Don't automatically assume that all professionals respond to the same kind of inspirational messages or that your ability to decide things quickly means that they are decided well. Watch for telltale signs that your high-energy style is rubbing people the wrong way. When you catch yourself in high-energy mode, turn down the flame. You're missing opportunities to use your Relating style; instead I'd like you to seek them out. Make an effort to listen to and learn from your people. Watch for chances to empathize and guide rather than offer high-octane encouragement.

Start by setting up meetings with each of your people to see how they are doing. Give them a chance to talk about any past accumulated frustrations. This will give you the information you need to be sure that your people support your mission and objectives and to deal with any issues they raise. It will open or reopen up the lines of communication. Prior to the meetings, reread Chapter Nine for reminders on attention and elaboration skills needed for listening and the tools for encouraging your people. If you have this meeting with each of your people and find that they are not open and forthcoming, you have some confirmation that you have been intimidating. You will need to prove to them that you are willing to listen better than you have in the past in order for them to trust that they can express themselves to you freely.

THE OVERWHELMER

You're over the top in more ways than one. You cannot work harder than you are already working. But this is not showing up in either the group's performance or the potential of your people to contribute and advance. I'm not questioning your contributions as an individual; they just don't translate into effective group management.

What is particularly bothersome is the way you use your intensity to control agendas, discussions, and time frames. In meetings, your people are often completely cowed, while you are aquiver with excess energy. In one-on-one interactions, too, you overwhelm people. Sometimes you try to get too close; other times you demand too much. The combination is highly intrusive; people feel like you're trying to "take them over."

You need to learn to moderate both your Requiring and your Relating tendencies but don't seem inclined to do so. Your intensity is at such a high level that it's difficult for you to dial it down; you seem to need it cranked up to function.

I would ask you to look at the following two lists of behaviors and choose the one that best describes how you currently act. Then carry this list around with you and post it everywhere: next to the phone, on your bulletin board, as a screen saver on your computer. After making the list of behaviors ubiquitous, vow to catch yourself when you're starting to exhibit one of these behaviors, and shut the behavior down.

Group A

- I take over in meetings; I interrupt other people and finish their sentences.
- I push others too hard—often to attempt the impossible.
- I am stubborn and refuse to change my mind.
- I prevent others from speaking out or volunteering ideas.
- I act in a highly directive manner, as if I know what should be done in every situation.

- I tell others my agenda while remaining uninterested in theirs.
- I confront people using harsh, strong, or judgmental language.
- I am insensitive to others' feelings.
- I'm arrogant about my own abilities and opinions.

Group B

- I believe I am responsible for my employees' success or failure.
- I have such a great need to be liked that I find myself trying to please employees on every interaction.
- I continually ask direct reports how they feel and if everything is OK.
- I am so empathic and understanding about how it feels to be confronted about performance issues that I avoid confrontations.
- I delegate to a fault, leaving employees on their own.
- I am accommodating and nice at the expense of getting quality work out on time.
- I have a tough time defining priorities.
- I allow people to change my mind by giving me more information or by expressing how much they want me to go in a certain direction.
- I look for direct reports' reactions just about every time I talk to them.

Most overwhelmers find that group A is more representative of their behavior than group B. It may be that you're really an energizer who takes the initiative to talk to your people, shares easily with them, and feels close to them without realizing that you are violating a space boundary and missing clues that your people want you to retreat a little. If, however, you're a true overwhelmer—someone who has an unusual excess of both Relating and Requiring behaviors—the best thing you can do is focus on your more natural style and try to shut down some of the excesses.

THE 2R MANAGER

I think you are doing a great job. I've seen you confront people in your group when it was clear they needed to be held accountable for mistakes, but I've also watched you empathize with direct reports who just needed to vent about a problem. You generally seem to know when to relate and when to require, and as a result, your group performs at a high level and your people are developing quickly and are likely to fulfill their potential. Though you have a natural style, you don't lean on it too heavily. You're astute about people and situations, and you consciously choose the style that is appropriate. You're quick to distinguish who in your group needs to be pushed and who needs to be listened to and encouraged and when. You also are able to shape your style to fit the parameters of an assignment. When a task or project has tight deadlines and ambitious goals, you're not afraid to push your team. When a task provides the opportunity for learning and growth, you're willing to sit down with individuals and allow them to question, take risks, and reflect on errors.

To realize your full potential, continue to be an astute observer of human behavior. With the skills you have, the more you understand, the more you will be able to accomplish. You will leave a legacy of people who will grow into management roles themselves and contribute to the success of the organization. You have a great future with this company; in the coming months, as higher-level positions open up, you'll be a prime candidate for them.

Whether you fit one of the nine types perfectly or recognize parts of your style in several of them, you should have a pretty clear picture of how you now manage your people, the impact you probably have on them, and what actions will help you become a more versatile and more effective manager.

CHAPTER THIRTEEN

The Benefits: For You, Your People, and Your Organization

Most of us know we can improve how we manage but don't make the effort to specify exactly what skills we need to develop and then go out and develop them. We are passive rather than proactive. We take the courses our companies provide us in project management, communication skills, diversity training, and so on. We may get some guidance from our managers in our first few years of managing, but this feedback seems to dwindle over time. We may pick up a book if it is a quick read on a management subject that interests us. The fact is that most managers aren't growing very quickly. If they are growing at all, it is in ministeps—incremental improvements as knowledge and experience increase. Becoming a 2R manager, however, is not incremental. It is a giant step up to another level.

When you put the lessons of this book into practice, you will become more than a manager who can use his less natural skill every now and then. Being able to use your less natural R is a key goal, but it is not the only one. As a 2R manager, you will find that you've grown and developed in many ways; you will have moved closer to the ideal of what a manager can be rather than the reality of what most managers are. Just as significant, you'll discover that your new skills and attitudes will serve both your career and your organization well in the changing environment of the twenty-first century.

Let's start out looking at the broader skills and perspectives you'll acquire as a 2R manager.

REDEFINING YOUR ROLE

Managers who have access to both Rs possess some powerful traits.

Self-Awareness

As you read about how to develop your Relating and Requiring skills, you probably noticed the underlying theme of being highly conscious of your managerial behaviors. People who are overly dependent on one R often operate from instinct. They don't reflect on who they are or what they do as a manager, their strengths and weaknesses. As a result, they don't undergo any self-examination that allows them to identify what they're doing right and what they're doing wrong and to improve their performance on the basis of this knowledge.

The 2R process is one of continuous self-examination. It fosters self-awareness by asking people to monitor their actions and think about the repercussions. Learning to use your less natural style and reduce dependence on your natural one demands that you be attuned to your motivations and goals as a manager. Knowing your demons and drivers becomes a tremendous advantage in that you can control them rather than letting them control you; you're able to respond to a situation based on the right thing to do rather than what you're unconsciously driven to do.

Aware of Your Impact on Others

As a 2R manager, you're not just self-aware but also aware of how your style affects the people you manage. Too often, managers are only dimly aware of their impact or delude themselves into believing that their impact is something it's not. Catherine, a natural friend type, was in the process of becoming a 2R manager. She felt that her people were intensely loyal to her because she had gone out of her way to develop a strong relationship with each of them. But Catherine also knew that her natural style had some negative impacts, so she wasn't overconfident that loyalty would be enough to hold her best people. She recently interpreted some complaints she received about roadblocks to getting work done as a softly worded criticism of *her* tendency to fail to set priorities and provide clear direction. She decided that the criticism was accurate, clarified what was needed most, and helped the group focus on its major tasks. She was able to pick up a clue she might have previously missed by being aware of her style's tendencies.

2R managers monitor how their actions affect others. Because they know their natural style and type, they possess prior knowledge of how they likely will affect their direct reports. As a result, they can anticipate what the negative reactions might be and can watch for telltale signs suggesting they need to modify their behavior.

Access to Alternative Behaviors in Specific Situations

One of the big jumps people make when they become 2R managers is that their responses are no longer limited to their particular style. As you have undoubtedly observed, some managers are terribly predictable in their behaviors. No matter who they're dealing with or the particular project they're working on, they manage within the same narrow range of responses.

2R managers recognize they have alternatives to this narrow range. They have learned that their natural style won't be effective with certain people and in certain situations. They understand that alternatives are available to them if they use their less natural style.

A Long-Term Perspective

Most managers view their role as managing a series of tasks and projects to accomplish specific objectives. 2R managers have an additional perspective: continually monitoring short-term actions to ensure that they contribute to long-term goals. They avoid expedient solutions that have negative future consequences. Each task or project is viewed not as an independent activity but as part of a process of making the next one easier. They work to build solid working relationships *over time*.

Trustworthiness

It isn't a secret that professional workers today are increasingly distrustful of management or that mergers, layoffs, executive compensation, bankruptcies, and other factors have created a cynical attitude among many employees. Earning back that trust is difficult, but 2R managers are in a good position to do so. Their people recognize that 2R managers have reduced previous tendencies to over-relate and over-require and that they will use the appropriate style to solve a problem (rather than to ingratiate themselves or pursue some hidden agenda). Direct reports grasp that 2R managers listen to them for understanding and coach to help them grow, while at the same time insisting on excellence and pushing them to achieve it. In other words, they perceive 2R managers as straight shooters who have both the interests of the individual and the interests of the organization at heart.

PREPARING TO DEAL WITH A CHANGING ENVIRONMENT

By becoming a 2R manager, you are acquiring the capabilities necessary to function at a high level of effectiveness in a changing environment. Now and in the coming years, managers are going to have to deal with all sorts of conflicts and complications that they never had to worry about before. For instance, how does a manager run a virtual team? How does she handle brilliant MIS people who may have non-traditional work styles but possess vital knowledge about a growing area of the company? How can a manager learn to manage relationships across functional boundaries and with "outsiders" who are part of a rapidly expanding, informal network of allies? Everything from outsourcing trends to matrix-structured organizations to e-commerce is thrusting managers into unfamiliar situations.

To handle these situations effectively, 2Rs are better than 1. Until relatively recently, managers with limited versatility could survive in organizations because they settled into a comfortable routine of familiar tasks. In recent years, however, the performance bar has been raised and the range of issues has broadened. One day, a manager may be attempting to resolve a conflict between two team members who are twenty years apart in age and have very different work and life values. Another day, she may be trying to help a direct report who has a flex-time arrangement with the company complete a project from his home. On still another occasion, she may need to advise a direct report who has been offered a job at another company about career opportunities within the organization and why he can realize his career goals if he stays.

Managers with access to both Rs are in a good position to handle anything they face. Top management will come to realize that this capacity is crucial if they want to generate better results and attract, develop, and retain their talent.

THE NEED FOR MORE
2R TOP EXECUTIVES

If you aspire to be a CEO or to be selected for any top management position, having 2Rs is your best credential. Let's look at why this qualification will be so important for leaders in the coming years.

Much has been written about the rising failure rate among CEOs. Analysis of the problem has revealed a number of explanations, from poor CEO selection processes to the increasingly difficult nature of the job. No matter what the circumstances might be, the fact is that many CEOs who fail are 1R managers. Demanders, for instance, have often been named to the top spot because of their take-no-prisoners mentality and passion for getting results. These types, however, frequently have trouble winning the war for talent; their style often causes some of the best and brightest people to leave. At a time when human assets are considered as valuable as financial ones, demander CEOs often run into problems. They cannot build the consensus needed to move the organization forward. The same holds true for friends. Although they're less likely than demanders to be selected to run an organization, they are viable candidates in companies with "people-oriented" cultures. Unfortunately, their style is not in tune with an environment where investors are placing greater emphasis on quarterly earnings and significant competition can come from new companies formed yesterday.

Being able to relate and require and knowing when to do each gives CEOs a decided edge. They recognize when they have to shift the organization's efforts toward the development of people and when they need to focus on getting better work out of their staff and line managers. Perhaps more to the point, they have a broader range of options when facing difficult situations. Their responses aren't limited by their natural style. If productivity is down, they don't automatically respond with demands to boost it. They understand that there are times when they can use their Relating skills to coach people to higher performance levels or better communicate information and ideas that will help employees perform better.

In addition, management is well aware that people tend to exhibit the behaviors modeled by CEOs. Any company that wants to increase its 2R managerial ranks recognizes that the place to start is selecting a 2R CEO. Managers close to the CEO always try to anticipate what he wants in order to give it to him. A Requiring CEO tends to be surrounded by a majority of Requiring managers in the ranks. If a Relating CEO is in charge, there will probably be numerous Relating managers. This is partly due to modeling and partly because CEOs influence the way training programs are set up and the types of behaviors that are rewarded. A Requiring CEO, for instance, will tend to focus training on productivity and financial factors, while a Relating CEO will make sure that managerial training includes a coaching component. A 2R CEO, by contrast, will understand the importance of training people to promote versatility and compensating those who achieve it.

To ensure that more organizations are run by this type of leader, more boards of directors need to make both Rs a "spec" in the CEO selection and succession processes. Boards select CEOs to lead in the best sense of that term: to create a vision for where the company needs to go and direct everyone's energies toward getting there. 2R CEOs are inherently more objective, visionary thinkers than 1R CEOs. Not only can they analyze problems and opportunities without bias, but they can also see farther and more deeply. Boards are well aware that companies are struggling to reconcile opposing needs. They want to achieve great results while at the same time adhering to organizational and social values. They want to provide the best possible customer service yet reduce costs wherever possible. While implementing a strategy that helps ensure the company's long-term success, they need to deliver strong quarterly earnings. 2R CEOs have the best chance to reconcile these competing agendas.

The need for CEOs with access to both Rs was made starkly clear on September 11, 2001. The skills needed to deal with the human elements of profound grief and subsequent fear and concern, while immediately mobilizing forces to secure and protect employees and facilities, spanned the widest range possible. The business world changed that day. Leadership since September 11 has never needed versatility more.

HOW TO BECOME A 2R EVANGELIST

Perhaps you've done an informal assessment of your team, department, or company and discovered that few people qualify as 2R managers. Although such a discovery may be disconcerting, it's by no means catastrophic or even unusual. Increasing the 2R capacity of any group of people is relatively straightforward. The principles of this book can be incorporated into just about any leadership development or manager training program. They can also be applied in less formal ways via coaching. As I noted earlier, one of the great advantages of the 2R model is its simplicity. People grasp the concepts quickly and can incorporate changes in their managerial style without a great deal of handholding or personal coaching.

What can you do to increase your group's 2R capacity? Consider putting some of the following ideas into practice:

Every manager should know the natural R and specific type of each of his managerial reports (and the inclinations of his nonmanager reports).

Whether you're the CEO or a first-time manager, you should know this basic information about your direct reports. Not only will this knowledge enable you to be a better manager, but it will also help you develop your people on a 2R path. Even if you're managing people who don't hold managerial positions, you can get them (especially the ones with high potential) on the right development track early. If, for instance, Marisa has a pleaser approach to her relationships, you know you have to help her learn to become more assertive before she is ready to be a manager. If Jim has a supervisor mentality, you know he will gain by learning to involve and listen to others better.

Training and coaching should focus on increasing versatility.

If you're an HR person, you can work toward making Training 101 a versatility-enhancing prerequisite for all managers. If you're a manager, you can coach with an eye toward encouraging and motivating people to be more versatile in their behaviors. Currently, managers and trainers are trying to convey so many different topics that it becomes an uphill climb. They are dealing with the right issues—getting people to produce better work and helping them develop their skills—but they're going at it in a laborious fashion. If all managers simply made a commitment to help their people become more versatile, all sorts of other goals would be achieved much faster. When managers and their direct reports are more versatile, they do everything from build teams to make decisions more effectively.

Managers should speak in 2R terms.

Poor communication is a barrier to both performance and development. Some managers don't develop a 2R style because their bosses never clearly communicated what aspects they needed to work on. In any organization, managers find it tremendously difficult to explain to direct reports what they're doing wrong. The 2R lexicon provides a communication shortcut, helping people understand how they need to change their behaviors without the complexity or negative connotations that usually accompany such discussions.

Rewards and recognition should be linked to versatility increases.

Though you may not be in a position to restructure your organization's reward and recognition system, you can certainly add some aspects to how you recognize and reward your people. Verbal pats on the back for attempting to increase Requiring or Relating behaviors are easy for managers to do. Performance reviews can include a versatility assessment (you can adapt the questions from Chapter Two to apply to nonmanagers). In the end, versatility improvement will result in better performance, promotion opportunities, and career alternatives, all of which provide greater economic rewards. There should be a strong economic motivation to become 2R managers.

MAKING THE 2R MODEL PART OF YOUR DAILY MANAGEMENT ROUTINE

Helping yourself and others become 2R managers is a process. It may be faster than others you've encountered in management training programs, but it still takes time. As you attempt to apply the ideas of this book to the realities of your work life, you may encounter resistance. You may find it difficult at first to use your less natural style consistently. You may also discover that this less natural style doesn't seem to have the effect you want it to have with certain direct reports.

Don't be discouraged by whatever resistance you encounter. People who become 2R managers make a commitment to push through this resistance, to keep focused on developing the versatility that will make them infinitely more effective. Most progress in personal growth is achieved by continually taking two steps forward and one step back.

Keep the benefits in the forefront: this is the best thing you can do for your organization and your career. When you hit a roadblock, remind yourself that by persisting, you will elevate yourself to a higher managerial level. Achieving the versatility, self-awareness, sensitivity, situational flexibility, and trustworthiness of a 2R manager is worth the effort.

As you finish this book, make a vow to manage your people better. Starting right now, think about each of your direct reports, and answer the following question:

> Do I need to ask, listen and understand, encourage, nurture, compliment, assert, or require in order to help this person achieve more?

You now possess the knowledge necessary to answer this question and to put the answer to work for you and your organization.

—᷍᷍— More Resources for the 2R Manager

This section offers some tools and techniques on three issues to further assist you in becoming a 2R manager:

- Getting feedback
- Finding time
- Disagreeing nicely

GETTING FEEDBACK FROM OTHERS

As managers, we will never know with any precision how well we are doing with our people. There are no completely objective measures. We must rely on a lot of subjective information, including our own opinions, feedback we get from our direct reports and our managers, quantitative results compared to objectives, general feedback surveys that the human resource department might conduct, and anecdotal information when someone leaves the company. Managers should be open to hearing information from all sources, but in the end, they must learn to be comfortable with a certain lack of absolute clarity about how well they are doing. With that preamble in mind, here are some thoughts about getting feedback from your employees and your boss about your relating and requiring leanings.

Getting Feedback from Your Employees

The following survey will help you confirm your belief about how you are coming across to your people. Think of it as a confirmation tool rather than an assessment tool. The opinions of people who report to you contain some inherent biases. For example, they may not trust that the information will remain confidential or may want to avoid giving you feedback that you might view negatively. Some may see you differently from others because you have indeed interacted differently with them. With those hedges, the following survey can be used to help you verify how your employees see you.

A SURVEY FOR YOUR EMPLOYEES TO COMPLETE

To: (Employee Name)

I am reading a book that looks into my management style. As I was taking some of the tests in the book, I kept thinking that I needed to ask you for your input. I would appreciate your completing this survey. Thank you in advance.

This survey consists of twelve statements about management activities. For each statement, I'd like you to indicate how you feel I perform that activity by rating the statement from 1 to 10, using the following scale:

1	2	3	4	5	6	7	8	9	10
Never		Seldom		Sometimes			Usually		Always

1. Relates to employees easily. _____

2. Includes employees in decisions. _____

3. Listens to employees. _____

4. Empathizes with and understands employees. _____

5. Encourages and compliments employees. _____

6. Shows a need to be liked by employees. _____

7. Insists on high performance standards. _____

8. Sets clear priorities. _____

9. Is comfortable making demands of employees. _____

10. Addresses performance problems quickly. _____

11. Is comfortable with disagreements and conflict. _____

12. Creates a sense of urgency. _____

Please send your responses to (*fill in the name of someone they and you trust*), who will keep the individual responses confidential and will summarize the average score on each question for me.

Your responses will be used to confirm or contradict information I have from other sources. All of these questions are designed to help me better understand the effects I have on the people I manage. Thanks for your responses.

INTERPRETING THE RESULTS. The first six questions concern Relating, and the last six concern Requiring. Ask the person who receives the completed surveys to calculate the following:

• The average score for each question from all respondents
• For each respondent, the sum of questions 1–6 and 7–12

These numbers can be given to the manager, with no names associated with the results. The manager can then determine whether he or she scored higher in Relating or Requiring and how he or she fared on each question.

Getting Feedback from Your Boss

Depending on how open your relationship is, I think you could ask your manager to complete either the same survey used for employees or the original surveys you completed. Whether you choose to do this will probably be determined by how much you would trust the results. For example, if you tested to be a friend type of manager, but would like confirmation, you may choose not to ask it of a demander boss but might be very comfortable with an energizer that you trusted. At some point in your development, it would be good to have an open discussion with your manager to be sure you understand how your Requiring and Relating skills are being appraised. The form used to survey employees could be used to facilitate such a discussion.

Getting Feedback As You Become More Versatile

As Relaters make changes to become more assertive, they would benefit from finding someone to reinforce what they are doing and to give them a reasonably objective assessment. This can be a manager, especially if the manager is also a Relater, or a direct report who will give honest assessments of progress, assuming that you trust that the exchange will remain confidential. Another option is to seek feedback from all your people. If you're a pleaser, I think feedback from every report isn't the most reinforcing, as you need to work on both Rs. If you're a friend, both of these options are available.

Requirers are more likely not to feel as great a need for ongoing feedback to stay the course. They will tend to rely on their own instincts for how well they are doing. For this reason, I think it might be best if they reused the employee survey, perhaps every six months or annually, to obtain formal feedback. As you make changes, it is important to learn how your employees are receiving them. At some point, it is also wise to connect with your manager and have an open discussion of what you are trying to do and how well you are doing it. Again, the form used to survey employees can be used to facilitate such a discussion.

FINDING TIME TO MANAGE

How can you find the time to manage when you can barely find the time to get your work done? This is the most common question I get from managers. Here are some ideas.

You may already be spending enough time.

If your scores on the Relating and Requiring surveys total 15 or more, you are now spending a good amount of time managing. That is the equivalent of giving every item a score of 3—you do these things "regularly." So for many of you, the question is not how to find more time but how to use the time you are already spending more wisely.

Managing well takes less time than not managing well.

As with many sports, good head coaching is a matter of strong recruiting and solid preparation. The better the players, the better the head coach looks. The more the team has commonly understood goals, the more likely it is that those goals will be achieved. And the earlier appropriate expectations are set, the better the team will play together. In managing people, this translates to doing great recruiting, clarifying the mission well, and setting realistic expectations early. Get very good players, and keep them on the team. If you are spending time trying to keep dissatisfied people from leaving or retraining new people, you are spending much more time than you would have spent had you managed your people well in the first place.

Recruiting well is the great time-saver.

The greatest determinant of how much time you will spend in managing is whether you recruit very good people. Every hire who is less than very good will cost you many hours (sometimes hundreds of hours).

Good mission clarity and clear expectations focus the direct reports' energies.

Direct reports join your group wanting to please you. You need to tell them exactly what you expect of them. You will spend far less time correcting their work if you set clearer expectations right from the start. It is harder to tighten up after you have been loose than to lighten up after you have been tight. Setting clear expectations early is very important to the ease of managing and the time you spend on it.

A lot of the time you spend on managing is at someone else's initiative.

For many managers, much of the time spent managing begins when they are interrupted. This is one of the reasons some people don't like to manage. But the manager can feel in greater control of her time by taking the initiative to manage—setting expectations, clarifying the mission, sharing information, obtaining reactions to some of your ideas, asking people how an assignment is going or how they are doing, giving compliments, and so on. The more managing you can do on your time schedule by carving out time for it and putting it on your to-do list, the less time will be spent dealing with last-minute emergencies. You will also enjoy managing more; and when you enjoy something, time goes quickly and it doesn't seem like a chore.

Learn good time management habits.

Here are a few tips:

• Create a contact list. This is a simple but effective way to save time. How many times have you wanted to talk to someone about three or four items and forgotten one of them when you talked? Then you have to track him down again, often at some inconvenience for one or both of you. Don't let it happen anymore. Take a lined pad, and at the left, write the name of anyone you have something to say to. Then next to that name, write all the items you want to cover when you see her. When you think of another item, just add it on the same line. Carry this pad everywhere with you (a small notebook or a handheld electronic organizer would work as well). When you next see or talk to the person, glance at your pad to be sure you cover all the items you wanted to talk to her about.

• Use travel time together better—share something, ask something, plan something in advance.

• See if you can delegate some of your management tasks. For example, some teaching or orientation of new people can often be done by experienced people in your group who might love doing it. Also, can your secretary help you more? (If you have a good secretary, the answer to this question is always yes!)

• Keep "five-minute files," a manila folder for each person who works directly for you, including your secretary. Occasionally ask yourself what you can do to help each person grow, and whenever you get five minutes, jot down your ideas and put them in the folder. When traveling or waiting for meetings, you'll find a lot of five-minute downtimes.

• Determine who you can legitimately reinforce today for doing good work. Complimenting does not take a lot of time.

If your Relating and Requiring scores total 13 or less, you probably do need to spend more time on managing.

You are not actively managing enough. But you can use some of the ideas presented here to help you use your time more effectively.

Requiring managers feel under great time pressure to get more things done. They don't believe they will save time by slowing down and focusing more time on people. They don't waste much time now, and they fear that slowing down to take these additional actions will be wasteful. This makes them personally efficient but managerially inefficient. You should know by now that you need to slow down enough to allow others to help you more.

Relating managers feel under great time pressure to get their own work done and also give their direct reports enough attention. It feels like a conflict, and typically the manager's personal work will suffer the most. It is hard to give your own work priority when you feel responsible to and for others. You need to speed up the processes and focus more on getting your own tasks done. Trust others more to come to you versus always reaching out for them. Appreciate your own needs and value your desire to complete your own work. You aren't likely to go overboard and suddenly ignore them.

2R managers understand that time spent trying to keep dissatisfied people from leaving, rehiring those who have left, and training new employees is an enormous expenditure made just to get back to where you were. If the same amount of energy were poured into doing a better job of helping people grow and contribute, more employees would stay, and the results in terms of good work done would be far greater.

Balancing Work and Family

This subject is beyond the scope of this book, involving deeply personal and broad social issues that change with changes in the local, regional, and global economy as well as with individual needs. In some companies today, managers are working with entire teams who are telecommuting—"teams" that bring a new definition to the term because they spend so little time together. Many organizations are responding to the need for balance with creatively designed programs such as flextime, sabbaticals, shorter workweeks, and family assistance programs. But managers are often the worst offenders by setting poor examples for a balanced life. Perhaps two comments that directly relate to the manager's role might be helpful.

First, I would repeat that the time needed to manage well is less than the time spent to manage poorly. A good manager does the upfront things well: recruiting the best people, setting realistic expectations, establishing a trusting relationship, and so on. The time spent here is a good investment. Less effective managers spend their time on the back end: correcting work, managing marginal workers, firing or losing people, rehiring and retraining, and so on. 2R managers have more time to balance their lives.

Second, we all have more options for balancing our lives than we think we have. It is too easy to feel that you don't have any choice but to do what you have always done. But you have other very reasonable choices. Every day, illnesses, accidents, and epiphanies occur that reorder the priorities on work and family issues. It shouldn't take a life-threatening illness to make us reevaluate our choices. Would your life be that different if you devoted more time to your family? It is worth evaluating the trade-offs with a different mix of priorities, if for no other reason than confirming what you are now doing.

DISAGREEING WITH SOMEONE— IN A NICE WAY

These tips will help the Relater assert and help the Requirer disagree without being disagreeable.

Your tone of voice and facial expression betray your attitude.

If you consider what someone says (or the person who said it) stupid, your tone of voice and facial expressions will give you away. If you regard it merely as a statement that you disagree with, made by someone who has lots of good ideas, your tone of voice and facial expression will communicate, "Let's talk more about this." Which reaction do you think will be more helpful to your relationship?

Find out if you really disagree, and if so, define the disagreement precisely.

Ask enough questions to find out whether the disagreement is in the goals, the method to accomplish the goals, the assumptions you are making, the reactions you expect from some action, or something else.

If you disagree, do so kindly.

Give the employee the feeling that although you disagree, that doesn't mean you feel he is dumb to believe what he believes. It doesn't even mean he is necessarily wrong.

Don't just disagree; suggest alternatives.

Especially in problem-solving meetings, it is fashionable to disagree with a point being made without offering a constructive alternative idea or solution. This is not helpful. It brings meetings to a standstill. Every attendee of a meeting (not just the leader) has a responsibility to help the group find solutions.

Evaluate whether the disagreement leads to a different conclusion.

Sometimes people just like to argue. If the disagreement does not lead to a different conclusion, get off the issue. If you have to say something, say that you disagree with the point, but since you agree with the conclusion, let's move on.

Recognize that you can be wrong in disagreeing and that you may be misinterpreting an important piece of information.

Be willing to be convinced, and convey your willingness. After all, you expect others to be willing to be convinced by your arguments.

Don't make a habit of being a disagreeing person.

Don't speak only when you disagree; make it known when you agree as well. Your disagreeing will carry much more weight if you also have a reputation of agreeing with others. And affirming people is an important part of a good relationship in which you can disagree.

~~~ References

Blanchard, R., and Johnson, S. *The One Minute Manager*. New York: Morrow, 1982.

Carlson, R. *Don't Sweat the Small Stuff—and It's All Small Stuff*. New York: Hyperion, 1997.

Carlson, R. *Don't Sweat the Small Stuff at Work*. New York: Hyperion, 1999.

Hunsaker, P. L., and Alessandra, A. J. *The Art of Managing People*. New York: Simon & Schuster, 1986.

Levering, R., and Moskowitz, M. *The 100 Best Companies to Work for in America*. Reading, Mass.: Addison-Wesley, 1984.

Nichols, M. P. *The Lost Art of Listening*. New York: Guilford, 1995.

Phelps, S., and Austin, N. *The Assertive Woman*. Atascadero, Calif.: Impact, 2000.

~~~ Recommended Reading

On More Effective Listening

The Lost Art of Listening, by Michael P. Nichols. New York: Guilford Press, 1995.
Listening: The Forgotten Skill, by Madelyn Burley-Allen. New York: Wiley, 1995.

On More Effective Asserting

The Assertive Woman, by Stanlee Phelps and Nancy Austin. Atascadero, Calif.: Impact, 2000.
The Assertiveness Workbook: How to Express Your Ideas and Stand Up for Yourself at Work and in Relationships, by Randy J. Paterson. Oakland, Calif.: New Harbinger Publications, 2000.
When I Say No, I Feel Guilty: Vol. 2, *For Managers and Executives,* by Manuel J. Smith. New York: A Train Press, 2000.
Did You Say Something, Susan? How Any Woman Can Gain Confidence with Assertive Communication, by Paulette Dale. New York: Citadel Press, 2001.

On Lightening Up

Don't Sweat the Small Stuff—and It's All Small Stuff, by Richard Carlson. New York: Hyperion, 1997.
Don't Sweat the Small Stuff at Work, by Richard Carlson. New York: Hyperion, 1999.

On Managing People

The Art of Managing People, by Philip L. Hunsaker and Anthony J. Alessandra. New York: Simon & Schuster, 1986.

First Among Equals, by Patrick J. McKenna and David H. Maister. New York: Free Press, 2002.

People Skills: How to Assert Yourself, Listen to Others, and Resolve Conflicts, by Robert Bolton. New York: Touchstone, 1986.

⎯⎯ Acknowledgments

I want to start by thanking Ted Hewitt, who founded Hewitt Associates in 1940. It was Ted's concept and sincerity about placing as high a priority on creating satisfying work experiences as on delivering excellence that first attracted me to the firm. Ted was looking for a successor (though he didn't tell me this at the time), when he hired me in May 1968, at age twenty-six, as his assistant. On January 1, 1970, I became the chief executive of Hewitt Associates. Not many founders would have given a young person so much opportunity so quickly. The firm succeeded by following his precepts, which eventually led to the Relating and Requiring concepts in this book.

I want to thank the various executive committees at Hewitt Associates. If there was ever a better relationship between the CEO and a board for twenty-three years, I do not know of it. Gerry Wilson and Dave Hunt allowed me to retire when I needed to, and for that I am grateful and healthy. I also want to add thanks to all the managers I worked with, who were open enough to give me the insights that are included here.

I want to thank my daughter, Jennifer Friedes, for her early comments and suggestions on organization. My stepson, Lev Kaye, and his wife, Eva, assisted in giving me reactions to the test questions. Lynn Trautman was very helpful with her insights on how *The 2R Manager* can work with existing training programs. Almost fifteen years ago, Rita Cashman put me in touch with my inner drive to write. She also reviewed an early edition of the book. Len Tenner helped me obtain reviews of the book.

Special thanks are due Bruce Wexler, who helped me organize, reorganize, and write some drafts of what is now included. David Maister has been one of my inspirations to write a book. He seems to do it so easily. No one understands professional service firms better than David, and his review of a late draft was incredibly helpful.

I want to thank the people at Jossey-Bass, including Julianna Gustafson and Kathe Sweeney, editors; Todd Berman, marketing manager; Erin Jow, marketing assistant; Tamara Kastl, editorial assistant; Jeff Wyneken, production manager; Jesica Church, publicity manager; and Bruce Emmer, copyeditor.

My deepest appreciation goes to my wife, Susan, who worked on this book with me every step of the way. Her encouragement, support, patience, new ideas, reactions, rewrites, edits, and final reviews were instrumental to its completion. (We both shudder to think how many times she had to remind me to match pronouns with antecedents.) More important, I just love being with her.

P.E.F.

~~~ About the Author

PETER E. FRIEDES received his bachelor's and master's of arts degrees from the University of Michigan and is a Fellow in the Society of Actuaries. From 1970 to 1993, he was the chief executive of Hewitt Associates, an international consulting firm in compensation, benefits, and human resources. He was chairman of Lake Forest Hospital in Lake Forest, Illinois; chairman of the Illinois State Scholarship Commission; chairman of the Jacob Blumberg Memorial Blood Bank; and one of the founding members of the Employee Benefits Research Institute in Washington, D.C. He has also served on the boards of the Ravinia Festival and the North Shore Blood Bank. Currently he is chairman of Valley Partners with California State University, a volunteer group that provides scholarships, tutors, and mentors to students in the Coachella Valley.

Friedes has always enjoyed talking to groups of young people, as a teaching fellow at the University of Michigan, a guest lecturer at Harvard Business School, a teacher at Northwestern's Kellogg Graduate School of Management, executive in residence at the University of Michigan and Emory University, and leader of hundreds of management courses at Hewitt Associates.

His passion is golf. Friedes started playing at age nine; won city championships in Rochester, New York, at ages fourteen and sixteen; and now competes in senior amateur events across the country. Since retiring, his handicap has dropped from 3 to 0.

Friedes lives with his wife, Susan, in Winnetka, Illinois, and winters in Indian Wells, California. They have four children, two grandchildren, and a third on the way.

Contacting the Author

I'm very interested in getting feedback from you. Many of you will have insights that could help modify or amplify my thinking and improve the next edition of the book. You can reach me via e-mail at pete@The2RManager.com. Please include your Requiring and Relating survey scores and any comments about your management type (or combination of types). I appreciate your willingness to share your thoughts with me.

PETE FRIEDES

⎯⤳⎯ Index